TORQUAY UNITED
50 Golden Greats

Other Desert Island Football Histories by Andy Riddle   ISBN

Plymouth Argyle: 101 Golden Greats   978-1-905328-64-3
Plymouth Argyle: The Modern Era (2nd edition)   978-1-874287-62-9
Plymouth Argyle: Snakes & Ladders   978-1-905328-34-5

TORQUAY UNITED
50 GOLDEN GREATS

Series editor: Clive Leatherdale
Series consultant: Leigh Edwards

Andy Riddle

DESERT ISLAND BOOKS

First published in 2009
by
DESERT ISLAND BOOKS LIMITED
7 Clarence Road, Southend on Sea, Essex SS1 1AN
United Kingdom
www.desertislandbooks.com

British Library Cataloguing-in-Publication Data
A catalogue record for this book is available from the British Library

ISBN 978-1-905328-63-5

Printed in Great Britain by the MPG Books Group, Bodmin and King's Lynn

The publishers acknowledge with thanks the following
for use of phtotographs in this book:
Leigh Edwards, Paul Hart

Contents

	Page			Page
1. Ralph Birkett	7	26. Ian Twitchin	79
2. Albert Hutchinson	9	27. Mike Mahoney	81
3. Don Welsh	11	28. Willie Brown	84
4. Ben Morton	14	29. Colin Lee	87
5. Bert Head	17	30. Les Lawrence	90
6. Ron Shaw	19	31. Steve Cooper	100
7. Dennis Lewis	22	32. John Turner	102
8. Sammy Collins	24	33. Colin Anderson	105
9. Don Mills	26	34. Derek Dawkins	107
10. Tommy Northcott	29	35. Kenny Allen	110
11. Eric Webber	39	36. Mark Loram	113
12. Ernie Pym	42	37. Tom Kelly	117
13. Geoff Cox	44	38. Jim McNichol	119
14. Terry Adlington	46	39. Phil Lloyd	122
15. Robin Stubbs	49	40. Lee Sharpe	124
16. John Benson	52	41. Dave Caldwell	128
17. John Bond	55	42. Matt Elliott	132
18. Bill Kitchener	58	43. Wes Saunders	135
19. Jimmy Dunne	61	44. Justin Fashanu	139
20. Alan Welsh	64	45. Darren Moore	142
21. Micky Cave	67	46. Don O'Riordan	145
22. Ken Sandercock	69	47. Tony Bedeau	148
23. John Rudge	72	48. Rodney Jack	151
24. Phil Sandercock	75	49. Kevin Hill	154
25. Mal Lucas	76	50. Chris Hargreaves	157
		List of Subscribers	160

Author's Note

'What's the title of the next book, Andy?'

'Torquay United: Fifty Golden Greats!'

I rarely finished my answer before being met with a look of incredulity, a raised eyebrow here, a frowned expression there. I knew what they were thinking. The poor old boy has lost the plot. Too many evenings in front of a computer in a darkened room I suppose. Fetch the white coats.

I guess the reaction was predictable. Throughout their history, Torquay have never set the footballing world alight. There has been the occasional promotion, cup shock, and play-off success, but generally they have loitered in the lower divisions and more recently been out of the Football League altogether. How could they possibly have produced 50 great players?

And so, I set about compiling my list of 50, a task, according to friends and family akin to climbing Everest backwards and blindfolded. I compiled my first 'short' list in what I thought was a ruthless fashion. This 'narrowed' my list to 130. Plan B – list the absolute certs to be included. Result – 78 players. A further cull was required.

I was overcome with guilt as the unfortunate 28 were struck through one by one. Mostly loyal and highly competent players who had given their all for the club dismissed at the stroke of a pen. Beheaded by the literary assassin.

Eventually my list was reduced to the requisite number. You will not agree with all my choices. We all have our favourites and so I apologise if yours is not among my selection, but I hope that it will prompt discussion, evoke memories and provide a few nostalgic moments.

A book cannot be produced without the assistance of a number of people and so I would like to acknowledge the contributions of Clive Leatherdale, my publisher, for again showing faith in my literary skills, soccer historian Leigh Edwards, and last but my no means least my wife Joy-Anne and children Sophie and Ben for their support.

No 1. **RALPH BIRKETT**

Debut: v Bournemouth, 8 March 1930
Farewell: v Northampton, 18 April 1933

During the course of its history, Torquay have always had a reputation for being unafraid to give local talent an opportunity. It is fitting, then, that our first 'great' was a local boy and certainly one of the best to emerge from South Devon.

Ralph James Evans Birkett was born in nearby Newton Abbot on 9 January 1913. His childhood was spent in Middlesex, where his promise on the soccer pitch saw him represent Woodthorpe School, Ashford and Middlesex Schools. On his return to Devon, he joined Dartmouth United where, despite his tender years, he soon gained a reputation as a skilful winger.

Word of Birkett's ability soon spread and it was no great surprise when he joined Torquay as an amateur when just 16 years old. These were uncertain times at Plainmoor. The club has only been in the Football League for two years during which time it had struggled both on and off the pitch. Financially, the club had been in a parlous state for several years and the opportunity for manager Frank Womack to sign players such as Birkett on amateur terms at least kept the directors and the bank manager reasonably happy.

The 1929-30 season had seen little upturn in playing fortunes. The side lost the first four games of the season although results gradually improved. Another devastating blow came in January, when a ferocious storm blew the roof off the grandstand. Already indebted to the bank, the club could not afford a replacement and the whole future of Torquay United lay in the balance. Local rivals, Plymouth Argyle and Exeter City offered to play fund raising friendlies and the world of football pulled together with donations flooding in from all parts of the country.

If the rest of the United Kingdom were trying to aid United's recovery, however, the players sadly weren't. Three successive 0-5 defeats hardly enticed extra punters through the turnstiles. By early March, Womack's rag bag bunch were still seeking their first win of the new decade. The manager was losing patience. For the home game against a Bournemouth side which had already inflicted both a 4-1 defeat in the league and knocked the Magpies (as Torquay were then known) out of the FA Cup, he recalled out-of-favour centre forward Joe Pointon. He also threw Birkett in for his debut on the right wing. The transformation was remarkable. Birkett had a dream debut, laying on four goals in a 7-0 thrashing. Pointon suddenly remembered what centre-forwards were supposed to do and scored four times. In fact, Bournemouth were let off lightly. Torquay also had four disallowed and missed a penalty!

The club quickly realised they had a gem on their hands and within two weeks, signed Birkett on professional terms.

The following season followed a similar pattern. Birkett was kept in the reserves for the first half of the season, the more experienced Scouser, Harry Waller being preferred in the No 7 shirt. A benevolent defence had again been largely responsible for another season of struggle and Birkett regained his place after a dismal run that had seen 25 goals conceded in just six games. Suddenly, United seemed a more cohesive unit and improved results saw them finish the season in eleventh spot, their highest finish since joining the League.

Injury aside, Birkett became a permanent fixture for the next two seasons, his fast powerful and direct style of play making him a feared opponent amongst lower-league opposition. It soon became obvious that his talents deserved a bigger and better stage than the ramshackle Plainmoor and, sure enough, that opportunity presented itself when Arsenal signed him for £1588 in April 1933, providing, at the same time, a welcome boost to the Torquay coffers.

At that time, the Gunners were the dominant side in English football under the tutelage of legendary manager Herbert Chapman, and Birkett seemed assured of honours. He did not have to wait long, winning a League Championship medal in 1934 and being a member of two Charity Shield-winning sides. Despite being a regular scorer when he did play, Birkett found his opportunities limited. He had been signed partly to replace fellow flankman Joe Hulme, who was in his thirties, but Birkett's capture only served to inject new life into Hulme who was largely preferred.

Frustrated by this, Birkett moved north, signing for Middlesbrough for £5,000 in March 1935. In October of that year, after an excellent performance in an international trial match, he was selected for the full England side who beat their Northern Irish counterparts 3-1 at Windsor Park, Belfast.

Birkett became a star at Ayresome Park, scoring an impressive 35 goals in 93 league appearances and twice being selected for the Football League representative side. In July 1938, a fee of £5,800 took him to Newcastle but fifteen months later war broke out. Birkett was just 26 and the conflict was to rob him of potentially his best years.

He joined the Army and became a Physical Training instructor. Birkett served in India but also managed to fit in a number of his games whilst back in 'Blighty', guesting for Darlington, Fulham, Chester, Middlesbrough, Chelsea and Reading, playing in one England wartime international in 1941, a 2-3 defeat by Scotland at Newcastle.

When war ended, Birkett was almost 33. He managed one more poignant appearance for Torquay during the 1945-46 interim season before the Football league officially resumed.

Birkett settled back in his native South Devon for the remainder of his days and was always cheerful and willing to talk about his career.

He passed away at Brixham in 2002 at the age of 89.

Magic Moment: *Birkett made an emotional return to Middlesbrough in 1995 when he was paraded in front of the crowd as Boro's oldest surviving player, receiving a tremendous reception.*

Worst Nightmare: *Following his England debut, Birkett impressed sufficiently to be selected for the next international against Germany, but was injured and replaced by a certain young Stanley Matthews, and never played for his country again.*

TORQUAY RECORD	Appearances	Goals
Football League	95	19
FA Cup	3	1

No 2. **ALBERT HUTCHINSON**

Debut: v Newport, 30 August 1930
Farewell: v Swindon, 6 May 1939

Albert Hutchinson was a Yorkshireman who went on to give excellent and loyal service to United, playing in a number of outfield positions during his career.

Sheffield born in 1910, 'Hutch' was a cutlery warehouseman who started playing junior football in the Sheffield area for the All Saints Old Boys in 1926. He quickly began to break all sorts of scoring records, notching 50 goals in his first season and 70 in the following campaign.

The 1928-29 season saw him join another Sheffield side, Atlas and Norfolk, who competed in the Drake and Intermediate League of the Sheffield Works Sports Association. Hutchinson's form made his two previous seasons look drought-ridden, as he notched an incredible 135 goals in just 26 matches, twice scoring fourteen in one game. Such statistics suggest that perhaps the standard of football was not the highest, but a goal tally of that magnitude in any form of football is impressive and it was enough to lure several league clubs his way.

Surprisingly, it was Luton Town who tempted him south. A goal a game in five reserve-team outings earned him a first-team place but Hutchinson was never initially able to fully adjust to the higher level and he managed only five games and one goal for the Hatters.

Keen to strengthen his squad, Frank Womack brought Hutchinson to Torquay in time for the commencement of the 1930-31 season, adding to a number of other signings and forming what was regarded as the club's strongest squad to start a Football League season. Hutch's favoured No 9 shirt went to another new boy, Jimmy Trotter, who also had Sheffield connections, having been signed from Wednesday, so Hutch had to settle for a place at inside-left.

The season began in encouraging fashion, but a bizarre run of inconsistency derailed any hopes of a promotion challenge. The forwards had few problems in scoring, but defensively United were erratic at best. Hutchinson, Trotter and fellow inside forward, Bill Clayson scored 51 goals between them, with Hutchinson and half-back Bob Smith playing every game to become United's first 'ever presents'.

An encouraging eleventh-placed finish augured well for the new season, but it started disastrously with a 0-7 opening-day defeat at Crystal Palace. It got worse. A 3-6 home loss to Watford was followed by a 2-10 annihilation at Fulham. Inevitably, manager Womack began to tinker with his line up. Leading scorer Jimmy Trotter was sold to Watford, with many calling for Hutchinson to lead the line, given his early scoring exploits. But there was more to Hutch's game than scoring goals, and he had developed into a creative playmaker with two good feet. He was used at wing-half and also at centre-half in another ever-present season.

Such results had led to the inevitable dismissal of Womack and trainer Frank Brown promoted. Brown restored Hutchinson to his more familiar inside-forward role for the 1932-33 season and was quickly rewarded for his decision, with 'Hutch' scoring a hat-trick in an 8-1 win over Southend.

Eventually appointed captain, Albert continued to give Torquay fantastic service right up to the war. He was a model of consistency, only missing the occasional game through the inevitable injury that was inflicted on him by the roughhouse tactics regularly employed by 1930s' lower league defenders. His versatility was demonstrated during his final season of 1938-39, when he spent much of his time in the left-back role, a position he had briefly flirted with a few seasons earlier.

The onset of war saw Hutchinson return to his native Sheffield to work in the steel industry. He was just 29, and the war feasibly robbed him of another five years of his career, when he could easily have notched up another 200 appearances.

Back in his home city, he worked for Firth Brown Steel before moving onto the English Steel Company and finally Richard W Carr Ltd. He epitomised the northern working class hero, bringing up his two sons with his wife Hilda, enjoying an occasional flutter on the horses and a drink with his friends. At least he could reflect on how his early scoring exploits had led him to the life of a footballer for a few years, an escape from the daily grind of a steel worker.

Albert passed away in May 1974 due to lung cancer.

Magic Moment: *Already United's longest serving player, Hutchinson's loyalty was rewarded with a benefit match against Norwich at the end of the 1935-36 season. Norwich won 3-0.*

Worst Nightmare: *Hutchinson was part of the United side that was sunk 2-10 by his former side Luton in September 1933. It remains Torquay's joint record defeat.*

TORQUAY RECORD	Appearances	Goals
Football League	317	15
FA Cup	15	2

No 3. **DON WELSH**

Debut: v Luton Town, 4 February 1933
Farewell: v Brighton 2 February 1935

United followers in the 1930s only had the pleasure of seeing Donald Welsh in action for two years, but he made a tremendous impact on the club and it was to be the start of a long and colourful career in the game.

Born in Manchester on 25 February 1911, Welsh joined United in an unconventional manner. As a regular in the Royal Navy, Welsh had been spotted playing for the Naval team at Devonport by Torquay boss, Frank Brown, having also played for Maltese side, Valetta. Brown was so keen to get his man that he offered to buy him out of the Navy. It all seemed fairly straightforward until Welsh admitted he was due to sail to China on *HMS Eagle* on a three-year commission.

The Navy agreed to release him, but with a proviso that Welsh had to find his own replacement. His search seemed in vain until the story goes that he struck up a conversation with a young man in a pub, whose long held ambition was to visit China. The deal was done, with Welsh allegedly giving his shoes to the youngster as a thank you.

Once ensconced as a footballer, Welsh did not take long in establishing himself in the first team after just two reserve games. Manager Brown was desperate to shore up a leaky defence that had conceded five goals on three occasions during the 1932-33 season, including the most recent game against local rivals, Exeter.

Welsh was thrown in at centre-half and made an immediate impact. United lost just three further games (one when Welsh was injured) and conceded just eighteen goals in the final seventeen matches.

Skilful on the ball and with an ability to read the game that belied his inexperience, it soon became apparent that Welsh was bound for a greater stage than Plainmoor. He became the outstanding United player of his day and was idolised by the United faithful It was little surprise that in February 1935 he joined Third Division rivals Charlton for a record fee of £3,250.

Charlton were dominating the division and won the title at a canter. They were a side going places, and the following season, with Welsh appointed captain, they remained unbeaten at the Valley and finished runners up to Manchester United.

The momentum remained the following year as vast crowds descended on the massive Valley terraces to watch the best players in the country. The visit of Arsenal attracted a crowd of over 68,000 but Charlton were unfazed by their new-found fame and were beaten to the League Championship only by Manchester City.

Welsh, by this time, had become one of the most respected players in the league. The term 'utility player' was made for him. Charlton used him at half-back, centre-half, centre-forward and inside-forward, probably his most effective position, where his strong running made him a constant threat.

Welsh's athleticism belied his appearance. Premature balding made him appear at least twenty years older than he was, but not only was his appearance on the field deceptive, he also had the reputation of being a joker off it, occasionally bordering on the eccentric.

The Addicks were now acknowledged as one of the top sides in the country on a consistent basis, and Welsh's part in their success was rewarded with three England appearances, against Germany and Switzerland at left-half in 1938, and at inside-left against Romania in May

1939, when he scored in a 2-0 win. This was England's last game before the war.

Welsh was 28 when war broke out. He joined the Army as a company sergeant-major instructor, with such duties affording him the opportunity to continue playing for Charlton, captaining them to two successive War Cup finals in 1943 and 1944, the latter ending in victory.

The indifferent standard of wartime football was to Welsh's liking. He played nine wartime internationals, scoring twelve times, scored 100 goals for Charlton in 119 appearances and also guested for Liverpool on 40 occasions, scoring 43 times.

When post-war football resumed, Welsh was approaching the veteran stage but had maintained his fitness levels. He led Charlton to the FA Cup final in May 1946, but his side were heavily defeated 1-4 by Derby. Due to the scarcity of gold, the medals were made of bronze, the players also receiving a gold version some years later. The following season, Charlton struggled in the league but again reached the Cup final, this time triumphing over Burnley. The match was a dour affair and went to extratime but with six minutes remaining Welsh glanced a cross onto teammate Chris Duffy, who scored the winner.

It was a fitting climax to Welsh's prolonged spell as a Charlton player, where he achieved legendary status. He announced his retirement at the age of 36 but six months later was back in the game as manager of Brighton.

He remained on the south coast until March 1951, when he was appointed manager of Liverpool to replace George Kay who had been forced into retirement through ill health. It was a surprise to many outside Merseyside, but Welsh had been an extremely popular figure at the club during his wartime guest appearances, and he had wanted to join the club as a coach but Charlton, not surprisingly, retained him. He had achieved little at Brighton, apart from converting them from a bottom of the table Third Division side to a mid-table one, but the opportunity to manage such greats as Billy Liddell and Albert Stubbins was one he could not forego.

Welsh's arrival was a shock to the system. Kay was a man of few words who generally distanced himself from the players. Welsh's zany side had not disappeared. His party piece was walking on his hands, a trick he performed whenever the fancy took him. Many a hotel guest thought the circus had arrived in town.

The job carried pressure. The Reds were seemingly poised to challenge the big hitters of English football, Spurs, Wolves, Arsenal and Manchester United. There was money to spend and crowds were flocking to Anfield but Welsh's spell in charge was not considered a success. His first full season saw them finish eleventh, but progress was not maintained. The following campaign saw them slump to seventeenth and a humiliating FA cup defeat to Third Division Gateshead.

It got worse. The 1953-54 season was the worst in the club's history, finishing bottom and conceding 97 goals. Welsh stayed for two more seasons. He generally had the backing of the Liverpool supporters, but in the end the ambitious Reds' directors lost faith and, in May 1956, having failed to return them to the top division, Welsh suffered the ignominy of becoming the first Liverpool manager in the club's history to be sacked.

He returned to Devon, purchasing a hotel in Bovey Tracey, but in 1958 was appointed manager of Bournemouth. After two mediocre seasons he was dismissed in February 1961 following a string of poor results. In July 1963 he was placed in charge of Wycombe, then a non-league side, leaving them in November the following year when he made a popular return to Charlton to work in their administrative office.

Don Welsh passed away at Stevenage in February 1990.

Magic Moment: *Memories of Welsh were revived in June 2008 when his Liverpool contract was put up for auction. The contract was hand-written on a single sheet of paper stating Welsh's salary of £1,500 per annum and various bonuses.*

Worst Nightmare: *Welsh was the manager when Liverpool suffered their record defeat – a 1-9 drubbing at Birmingham in December 1954.*

TORQUAY RECORD	Appearances	Goals
League	79	4
FA Cup	5	0

No 4. **BEN MORTON**

Debut: v Queen's Park Rangers, 5 September 1936
Farewell: v Aldershot, 23 October 1937

Sadly, Benjamin Morton was not a Torquay player for long, but statistically he is one of the greatest goalscorers in their history. Had he stayed, who knows what records he may have set.

Like Albert Hutchinson before him, Ben Morton was also born in Sheffield in 1910 (28 August), but whilst Hutchinson started his football career in his home city, Morton's first taste of regular 'senior' football came in the Midlands with Stourbridge.

As a centre-forward, he became a prolific scorer and it was of no great surprise when he made the short journey to Wolverhampton Wanderers in February 1933. Wolves, however, were a First Division side and it soon became apparent to Morton that the gulf between them and his previous employers was vast and not one he had much chance of bridging. Within a short time he had returned to Stourbridge.

Unperturbed by this experience, Morton continued to score for a pastime and in May 1935, Manchester United manager Scott Duncan made a double swoop, signing Morton and his Stourbridge team-mate, Dick Gardner.

United were a Second Division side, but again Morton would play the role of understudy, this time to regular No 9 Tom Bamford. Welshman Bamford quickly deemed himself indispensable by scoring seven times in the opening six games of the season, but was injured for the home game against West Ham on 16 November 1935, and Morton was drafted in for his debut. The visitors ran out 3-2 winners and Morton was quickly back with the 'stiffs'.

This defeat was a rare one, as United stormed to the Second Division title. Morton never had another sniff of a first-team appearance and at the end of the season was allowed to leave, with Torquay manager Frank Brown snapping him up on a free transfer.

United, by their standards, had just come off the back of a reasonable season, finishing tenth. Morton was one of three new forwards signed, giving greater cause for optimism. Morton, however, was an unknown quantity. He had one league game under his belt and although Manchester United were a decent team, the signing of a Red Devils centre-forward not was one to cause the great excitement that it would generate in modern times.

Morton was omitted from the opening two league games, which reaped a solitary point. He was handed his Torquay debut in the third game and quickly settled into the team. His first goals came in his third game, a double in a 5-2 victory over Bristol City.

Despite Morton's impressive form, United's close-season optimism was in tatters. They were badly misfiring, scoring just twenty times in the first eighteen games. Morton was one of the few players justifying their place. The more games he played, the better he adapted to the rigours of league football. Morton could certainly handle himself. He was not particularly tall (5ft 10ins) but at close to 13 stone he was powerfully built and able to hold off defenders.

The second half of the season really saw him find his feet. He soon gained the tag of Torquay's 'star' player. The message was out. Stop Morton and you stop United but few teams did. He embarked on a rich vein of scoring form, and by the end of the season had scored 23 times in 37 league games, including a hat-trick against Aldershot. His team-mates scored only another 34 between them, in what proved to be a desperately disappointing campaign as United finished third bottom.

The hope was that Morton was not a 'one season wonder'. He soon proved he wasn't, finding the net regularly. In fact, United's season got off to a reasonable start, winning five of their first eleven games, but the following game, a disastrous 1-5 home defeat by Aldershot, was to be Morton's swansong.

His twelve games had yielded ten goals, but also made him one of the club's biggest assets. So, when divisional rivals Swindon came along dangling a cheque for £1,000, it was an offer the cash-strapped Plainmoor directors could not refuse.

Morton's departure coincided with a dreadful downturn in results. There was no one to take over the scoring mantle, and in the 30 games after his departure, Torquay managed a measly twenty goals. To highlight the scoring plight, Morton's tally still made him the club's top scorer.

In contrast to his Torquay form, Morton took time to settle at Swindon, failing to score in his first ten games. It was not what the Wiltshire fans expected from someone who, at that time, was their club's record signing.

He eventually broke his Swindon 'duck' by getting a late equaliser to send an FA Cup-tie with Grimsby into extra-time but finished the season with just seven goals from 33 games for his new club.

The following season, he regained his scoring touch with some aplomb, notching 28 league goals, including three hat-tricks, to make him the leading scorer in Division Three (South), as well as getting three FA Cup goals.

As with many, the war effectively ended his career. He managed one game for Swindon in 1945-46 before returning for a third spell at Stourbridge where he ended his career.

Magic Moment: *In only his seventh Torquay appearance, Morton scored a rapid hat-trick in a 5-0 Division Three (South) Cup win over Northampton.*

Worst Nightmare: *Four months after leaving Torquay, Morton returned to Plainmoor with his Swindon side. He was afforded a great reception but failed to score and ended up on the losing side.*

TORQUAY RECORD	Appearances	Goals
League	49	33
FA Cup	1	0

No 5. **BERT HEAD**

Debut: v Aldershot, 7 November 1936
Farewell: v Plymouth Argyle, 7 October 1950

It is fair to say that Bertram James Head is best remembered for a successful managerial career, but as a player he was a Torquay stalwart and the mainstay of their defence for many years.

Born in the Somerset town of Midsomer Norton on 8 June 1916, Head began his playing career with his local side before moving to a better standard of football with Welton Rovers. He signed for Torquay in October 1936 and a month later was thrust into the team for his debut at right-back following an injury to Reg Parker, forcing Freddie Green the regular incumbent of the No 2 shirt to switch to left-back.

Head made intermittent appearances during that season and for the start of the following campaign again found himself playing in the reserves. Following the departure of prolific centre-forward Ben Morton and the subsequent goal-famine that followed, Head was asked to lead the line for a few games, scoring a couple of times.

The start of the 1938-39 season saw Head back in his favoured No 2 shirt, Green having transferred to Brighton. His consistency saw him play every game and scoring once in a rare foray upfield.

After the war, Head found himself back at Plainmoor and appointed captain. He switched to centre-half, where he was again a model of consistency, despite being not particularly tall for a central defender, his reading of the game and calmness under pressure more than adequately compensating. Over the next three seasons, Head rarely missed a game and his outstanding service to the club was rewarded by a testimonial match in April 1947 against Belgian champions RFC Malinois. Foreign opposition was still a mystery to the British game and United were one of the first club sides to compete with a European counterpart. A healthy crowd gathered, somewhat quizzically but went home impressed by the skill of the Belgians, who ran out 3-1 winners.

Despite approaching the veteran stage, Head continued to be an almost permanent fixture in United's defence until time began to catch up with him. He eventually lost his place and the captaincy, but his league career had a mini revival when he joined Bury in February 1952, making another 22 appearances before taking up a coaching role at Gigg Lane.

Head also fulfilled the role of chief scout and assistant manager at Bury before joining Swindon as manager in October 1955. The Wiltshire club were struggling and a season later had to apply for re-election. With a non-existent transfer kitty, Head relied heavily on developing youth players with startling success. He was not the ranting, bawling type of manager. Indeed, quite the opposite was true. A kind, thoughtful man, he nurtured his kids through the ranks to produce a host of players who would become Swindon legends – Don Rogers, Mike Summerbee, Rod Thomas, Ernie Hunt and Roger Smart were just a few who went on to achieve great success in the game. Head's philosophy was if they were good enough, they were old enough. In a pre-season trial match in 1960, the 'Possibles', a team of youngsters, beat the more experienced 'Probables'. Head immediately promoted both 'Possible' full-backs, John Trollope and Terry Wollen, into the first team even though they were both just seventeen.

Another of his young recruits was his son, David. He failed to break into the Swindon team but later appeared for Reading and became manager of Trowbridge at the age of 23.

The performances of 'Bert's Babes', as they were known, transformed the fortunes of the club and in 1962-63 Head guided his side to their first ever promotion.

The following season saw his side win their first six games until their form stuttered and they finished mid-table.

A devastating run of injuries took their toll during the following campaign and Swindon suffered a final-day relegation. In the August prior to the start of the new season, Head was sacked, much to the disgust of many Swindon fans. He was not out of work for long, returning to Bury as manager in the same month, replacing Charlton-bound Bob Stokoe, where one of his first jobs was to sell the highly rated Colin Bell to Manchester City to raise much needed funds.

Head remained at Bury for just eight months before being 'head-hunted' by Crystal Palace, a team similar to Swindon in that they were short of funds. Again, Head worked his magic, leading them to top-flight football for the first time in their history in 1969, and, more importantly, keeping them there for the following three seasons, albeit it a constant struggle to avoid relegation.

In March 1973, with Palace again in the bottom three, the ebullient Malcolm Allison was brought in as manager, with Head gently moved aside into a general manager's role. Palace were still relegated and, with little future at Selhurst Park, Head left.

Returning to his native Somerset, Head had a spell as manager of Bath City, later becoming a director of the club. He also served Swindon again, using his vast knowledge of the game as a scout.

Head died in Reading on 5 February 2002 at the age of 85, a figure fondly remembered by the many people he dealt with during his lifetime in the game.

Magic Moment: *The opening game of the 1948-49 season saw Head given the task of marking the legendary Tommy Lawton. In incessant rain, the England centre forward barely had a kick as United ran out 3-1 winners.*

Worst Nightmare: *After a 4-7 thrashing by Watford in April 1936, a young Bert was brought in for the next game to strengthen the defence. The game against Brighton ended in a 1-5 defeat!*

TORQUAY RECORD	Appearances	Goals
Football League	224	6
FA Cup	14	0

No 6. **RON SHAW**

Debut: v Bristol Rovers, 18 January 1946
Farewell: v Aldershot, 8 March 1958

Ron Shaw was living proof that appearances can be deceptive. Short, bald and with an appearance more akin to a clerk in a solicitor's office, Ronald Shaw went on to become one of Torquay's longest serving and exciting players and his claims to be included in a tribute to the clubs greatest servants can surely not be questioned.

Born in the small Yorkshire village of Bolton-on Dearne on New Year's Day 1924, Shaw joined the Army during the Second World War. Serving in the Royal Engineers, he quickly attained the rank of sergeant despite his youth.

His skills on the football pitch also came to the fore during his Army career, to the extent that he was signed by Charlton as an amateur, but his opportunities were greatly restricted by his service duties and he made just one wartime appearance for the club (alongside Don Welsh.)

The manager tasked to lead Torquay into the first post-war league season was former player Jack Butler. Unsurprisingly, he had little money to play with, and was fortunate that several of the pre-war line up had returned to the club. The remainder of the squad were a mix of free transfers and almost free transfers.

One of those new signings was Shaw, who was signed from Harrow Town. Initially, he could not break into the first team, with Butler's mixed bag producing some surprisingly good results, but our man was given his debut at inside-right following two successive defeats.

It was a winning debut, United beating Bristol Rovers 3-0 with centre-forward Jack Conley, generally regarded as the best header of a ball ever to wear a United shirt, scoring a hat-trick. But even Conley's performance was overshadowed by Shaw's. The wee man gave a superb exhibition of close control, dribbling and superb crossing which immediately made him the new darling of the Plainmoor crowd.

Despite the introduction of Shaw into the regular line up, United's form slumped in the second half of the season. Shaw continued to excite but the team relied too heavily on Conley to score. The centre-forward ended up with 23 goals from 34 games as a mid-table finish was attained.

The following season saw Shaw take over the mantle of top scorer, as he notched seventeen goals from inside-right. Conley's form took a turn for the worse, but Shaw began a fruitful partnership with right-winger Dennis Lewis. Under new manager John McNeil, United were still an outside bet for promotion until a terrible run of form which saw them collect just two points from eleven games transformed them into candidates for re-election. The situation was not helped by an injury crisis. For the home game with Walsall, both of the club's keepers, Phil Joslin and Gerry Matier, were crocked and McNeil failed to sign a replacement, forcing outfield player Jack Casley to play between the sticks.

With yet another season of struggle behind them, it was all change for the 1948-49 season. Ten new players arrived during the summer, again mainly on free deals. The season would be a precursor to one of the more successful periods in the club's history, one which would several quality players make their mark at Plainmoor.

Conley regained his scoring touch, Shaw was again mercurial, and the upshot was a ninth place finish – Torquay's best to date. They also reached the fourth round of the FA Cup for the first time, beating Second Division Coventry on the way (a first ever victory over a higher division side) before succumbing to Brentford. It was a testimony to the way in which manager McNeil had moulded the side that became known as the £500 team.

This early post-war era also saw crowds flock to watch football. The September local derby against Exeter saw almost 14,000 cram into Plainmoor to set a new attendance record.

The final season of the 1940s was even more exciting. The regular forward line of Shaw – now permanently an outside-right, Lewis, Conley, Don Mills and left-winger Hugh Cameron is still regarded as one of the best the club has ever fielded. Shaw, dubbed the 'Wing Wizard' and Cameron had few peers as a wing pair in the lower divisions.

A victory at Nottingham Forest in mid-January saw them briefly assume top spot. They remained in the frame for promotion but the bid was derailed by the shock departure of McNeil in March. The manager left to take over at Bury, citing his main reason as the apathetic nature of the locals. He did not believe United could fulfil his ambitions on average home gates of eight and a half thousand!

A meagre three points from the final nine games led to a final position of fifth, but nevertheless gave great cause for optimism that the club would finally escape the clutches of the lower league.

Shaw was now a Torquay institution. Despite his seemingly fragile frame and the regular desperate tactics employed by his markers, he rarely missed a game. He would also regularly reach double figures for his seasonal goal tally. In 1951, he was rewarded with a testimonial against his former club, Charlton.

His avoidance of serious injury came to an end in January 1954 in a match at Exeter in which he scored what proved to be the winner. The injury kept him out for the remainder of the season. It was perhaps no coincidence that the team's form went to pieces from that moment, as another potential promotion campaign ended with only four wins from the final seventeen games.

The 1956-57 season saw United agonisingly miss out on promotion by goal-difference to Ipswich. Shaw was now 33, his best days behind him. Sadly, he would not get the chance to display his skills at a higher level. He damaged his right knee and was never able to fully recover. He made just eleven appearances in his final season before moving back into non league football with Tonbridge.

Ron Shaw would never be forgotten at Plainmoor, however. After his death in 1991, a memorial service was held at the ground attended by a number of his former colleagues and his ashes scattered on the pitch.

Magic Moment: *Despite a faltering promotion bid, Shaw scored Torquay's goal in a 1-1 draw at eventual champions, Notts County. United, and Shaw in particular, produced a superb performance in front of a crowd of almost 44,000.*

Worst Nightmare: *Shaw was called into manager Eric Webber's office to be told he was being left out of a floodlit friendly match against Blackburn, as Webber wanted to look at a 'youngster' he was going to play. The 'youngster' turned out to be the great Stanley Matthews, who had agreed to guest for Torquay.*

TORQUAY RECORD	Appearances	Goals
League	384	99
FA Cup	28	7

No 7. **DENNIS LEWIS**

Debut: v Aldershot, 23 August 1947
Farewell: v Coventry, 26 December 1958

Another of John McNeil's astute signings was Dennis George Lewis, a Welshman born in the small coal mining community of Treherbert on 21 April 1925. If a transfer fee had been involved, McNeil and Torquay would certainly have had value for money, but Lewis was another free transfer, arriving from Swansea.

Lewis had signed for Swansea in August 1946, a preferable alternative to an otherwise almost inevitable life down the mines. He failed to break into the Swans' first-team however, but exactly twelve months later was snapped up by McNeil, one of three new signings, the other two, Charlie Hill and Les Evans, coming from Cardiff.

Lewis was immediately thrust into the first team, at outside-right, for the opening game of the season against Aldershot and chose the best possible way to impress his new followers by scoring a second-half goal in a 2-0 win, aided by an injury to Shots keeper, Reynolds. Little did the fans know that they were witnessing the start of a long and loyal relationship with the club that would continue long after his playing days were finished.

Lewis's name quickly became one of the first on the teamsheet each week, mainly at outside-right, although he would regularly interchange with inside-right Ron Shaw, throwing opposition tactics into disarray. He would also chip in with his fair share of goals. Lewis endeared himself to the fans with his 100 per cent effort and commitment, but there was more to his game than that. He was skilful and had great vision, which was most effectively used later in his career when he was switched to wing-half.

Lewis's commitment and drive made him a natural leader and he was the obvious selection to be appointed captain. He was always a calming influence both on and off the field and a model professional. His selection in the No 4 shirt for a game at Colchester in November 1952 started a remarkable sequence of appearances which saw him appear in every game until Easter 1957 – an unbroken run of 220 league and cup matches. During that time he was also awarded a testimonial against Cardiff.

Lewis was quickly back in the fold adding to his mounting tally of appearances, but after the Boxing Day clash with Coventry in 1958, he succumbed to a knee injury and, with age no longer on his side, he retired from the game, having set a Torquay appearance record which subsequently stood until 2008, when it was broken by Kevin Hill. Coincidentally, Lewis's final goal for the club was scored a few weeks earlier against Aldershot – the team he had scored his first goal against.

The injury was not enough to prevent him turning out for the reserves though, where his vast experience, knowledge and professionalism were put to good use, coaching the club's younger players. He was also offered a role within United's commercial department where he remained for several years, his reputation and popularity helping his role of fund raising for the club. In latter years, he became a billiard table fitter.

Magic Moment: *To mark his 300th game Lewis (and Ron Shaw) were presented with commemorative tankards before a floodlit friendly against Birmingham City.*

Worst Nightmare: *During a Third Division (South) match against deadly rivals Plymouth Argyle at Plainmoor in March 1957, Lewis attempted to hook a cross away from under his own crossbar, but the ball struck Argyle centre forward, Neil Langman, full in the face and went in for the equaliser.*

TORQUAY RECORD	Appearances	Goals
League	442	30
FA Cup	31	2

No 8. 'SAMMY' COLLINS

Debut: v Reading 2 October 1948
Farewell: v Newport 26 April 1958

There must have been regret from the decision-makers at Swansea when they studied the playing record of Dennis Lewis. The same could also be said for Bristol City, as they deemed Sammy Collins to be 'not good enough'. Collins' scoring record at Torquay should have left the Bristol City faces red with embarrassment at the decision.

The reason Collins was known as 'Sammy' was never really established, for he was named Ronald Dudley Collins when he was born in Bristol on 13 January 1923. To add to his identity crisis later in his career, he was dubbed 'Bill' by the popular side at Plainmoor.

Collins was brought up in the place of his birth and began to play soccer for local teams in the area. He showed great potential and signed for Bristol City in November 1944.

He developed well at Ashton Gate but always found himself on the fringes of the first team, accumulating just fourteen appearances with two goals so, in the summer of 1948, Collins, believing he had more chance of regular first-team football, joined Torquay for what was, in modern parlance, a 'nominal' fee.

He still had to show patience but, after some impressive reserve team appearance, was given his first-team debut when, after a dreadful 0-4 home defeat by Swansea, manager John McNeil made several changes. It was not an auspicious start, with United going down to another 0-4 defeat at Reading's Elm Park.

Collins, playing at inside-forward, soon settled into the side and showed an eye for goal, scoring thirteen times in just 22 appearances during his debut season to provide the perfect foil for centre-forward, Jack Conley (nineteen goals).

The following season was a similar story, with Collins occasionally injured, he finished as second top scorer to Conley (fourteen) with twelve strikes.

The enforced retirement of Conley through injury part way through the 1950-51 season saw Collins assume the mantle of Torquay's main source of goals, although he himself missed a chunk of the season through injury.

The following campaign saw Collins score 22 times in 42 games, a tally matched by his new forward partner, Ernie Edds, a pocket dynamo signed from Blackburn.

Collins was now firing on all cylinders. He was a feared opponent, his positional sense and eye for a half-chance accounted for many of his goals, but his most fearsome weapon was his speed off the mark. Few could match him over a five or ten-yard sprint, certainly not 1950s' Third Division defenders. Fitness was not top of a centre-half's priorities in those days.

In 1952-53, Collins scored 27 times, breaking the club's previous highest tally for a season, held by Jimmy Trotter in 1930-31, and also making the him club's all-time top scorer, overtaking Albert Hutchinson. His figure was aided by several penalties. No one would get the ball off Collins once a spot-kick was awarded. He missed just four times in his career. At the end of the season, he was awarded a benefit game against his former club, Bristol City.

By the end of September 1953, Edds had been sold to Plymouth, with striker Harold Dobbie making the opposite journey as part of the deal. Dobbie filled Edds' boots adequately, quickly settling in as Collins' new partner in crime. For Collins, the season almost represented a failure for he managed a 'mere' seventeen goals.

He was soon back on song for the following season, scoring 28 times. One of the most important was a second-minute goal against Leeds in an FA Cup third round replay. The 'Magpies', as Torquay were still known at that time, had managed a surprise 2-2 draw at Elland Road to force the return match. Leeds, including the famous John Charles, never recovered from Collins' early strike and found themselves on the end of a 0-4 hiding. Torquay's reward was a home tie with First Division Huddersfield, one of the top sides in the country. Much of the pre-match publicity centred on Collins and how he would strike fear into the hearts of the favourites. Clearly 'Health and Safety' did not exist in the 1950s, as almost 22,000 spectators somehow squeezed into Plainmoor, only to see Huddersfield score the only goal.

Collins' star reached its ascendancy in 1955-56. He was simply a goal machine, scoring an incredible 42 goals in 49 league and cup games. The tally included no fewer than five hat-tricks. He took a particular dislike to Walsall, scoring a trio in both games against the Midlanders. It was a tally that set a new scoring record for the club, and one which still stands today. Will it ever be beaten? Unlikely. Today's defences are more disciplined and the game more cautious, where not losing is the main priority. Collins' name is likely to be etched in United's history books for ever.

Despite the fact that he was a marked man in more than one sense, he continued to score goals as if it were a hobby. He made a real attempt on his own record but scored 'only' 35 goals in 49 games in 1956-57, helping United to second spot. There were two more hat-tricks to add to his collection, as well as scoring four against Millwall. Poor old Walsall were also on the receiving end. Collins scored a penalty against them after just ten seconds, after a long ball from the kick-off saw Ted Calland upended in the area.

What was more remarkable was that this golden spell was achieved in his thirties. Had he been five years younger, a move to a bigger club would surely have beckoned.

Sadly, Collins did not bow out on a high. Injuries and age began to take their toll during his final season. He managed to pass the 200-goal mark, however, before bidding a fond farewell to Plainmoor with a host of records under his belt. His tally of 219 goals still stands and is another record that will be a tough one to beat.

Collins joined Gloucester City, but returned to Torquay after his playing days were over to run a newsagents in Forest Road near the Plainmoor ground. On his retirement, he returned to live in Bristol, where he passed away in hospital on 31 May 1998, age 75.

Magic Moment: *In only his second game for Torquay, Collins returned to his former club, Bristol City, and scored in a 2-0 win at Ashton Gate.*

Worst Nightmare: *Later that season, City extracted revenge with a 2-0 win at Plainmoor. Collins was injured during the game and missed the next five matches.*

TORQUAY RECORD	Appearances	Goals
League	356	204
FA Cup	23	15

No 9. **DON MILLS**

Debut: v Brighton, 19 March 1949
Farewell: v Barnsley, 2 May 1962

Despite the phenomenal scoring record of Sammy Collins, it is Donald Mills who is generally regarded as the greatest of all United players.

The Gulls have been well served by Yorkshiremen over the years and Mills was no exception. He was born in Maltby near Rotherham on 17 August 1928. As with most young boys of his age, he seemed destined to work in the local colliery but, aged sixteen, he was spotted by a QPR scout playing at nearby Bramley. He was invited to Loftus Road and impressed sufficiently to be given a professional contract on his seventeenth birthday.

Despite his obvious ability, Mills was a pallid, frail teenager. Although 5ft 10ins, the official records of the time list his weight at only just over 10 stones. He was never a regular at Rangers but managed 48 appearances, scoring nine goals. In March 1949 he was loaned to Torquay, with the belief that a spell of sea air would help him develop physically. He was United's first ever loanee.

Mills slotted into the inside-left berth for the remaining ten games of the season, scoring four times, including a hat-trick in a 7-1 win over Leyton Orient. His arrival certainly coincided with a great run of form, which saw him taste defeat just once in those ten games, lifting United well clear of any threat of re-election.

Mills quickly made a huge impression at Plainmoor. He was a class act, possessing a cultured left-foot, superb control and creativity. His stock rose to the extent that the supporters, knowing the club could not afford to buy him, attempted to raise the money themselves. Their efforts were in vain and after another romp against Leyton Orient (4-1), in which Mills scored, he rejoined QPR in January 1950.

He played another 31 games for Rangers, scoring three times before a fee of £12,500 took him to Cardiff in February 1951.

The move to South Wales was not a happy one. Mills played just one league game and, in September of the same year, moved to Leeds, with Cardiff losing £500 on their original deal.

Many expected Mills to settle at Leeds, having returned to his Yorkshire roots, but memories of his ability and popularity at Torquay had not faded. After fifteen months at Elland Road, with another 34 league games and nine goals under his belt, Plainmoor boss Eric Webber broke the club transfer record in paying £5,000 to bring Mills back to United on a permanent basis.

The fans were overjoyed and certainly needed something to cheer them up. United were struggling near the foot of the table, had been unceremoniously dumped out of the FA Cup by non-league Peterborough, and just lost 2-7 at Coventry.

Mills was seen as the returning Messiah and did not let the fans down. He scored in his return match, a 4-2 win over Southend, and showed he had lost none of the skill he was remembered for.

Indeed, if anything he was a better player, having matured physically. His return coincided with an upturn in the team's fortunes which saw them finish in mid-table. Mills himself scored ten times in 24 games and his incisive passing created a host of chances for the irrepressible Sammy Collins.

Mills became an automatic choice in Torquay's No 10 shirt, combining consistency with some important goals. He was regarded by many as the best player in the lower divisions. Towards the end of the 1954-55 season, he was selected for a Third Division (South) representative side which played their northern counterparts in a match that was televised. The South won 2-0 with 'The Don' their outstanding performer.

After the euphoria of a second-place finish in the Third Division (South) in 1956-57, hopes were high of promotion in the following campaign, but in only the fourth game of the season Mills was the victim of a vicious tackle in a game at Gillingham and was forced to miss a large chunk of the season. His absence seemed to have a knock-on effect and in complete contrast to the previous year, United struggled to win a game.

It could be argued that Mills was never quite the same player after this incident. Injuries played a more significant part of each season.

United gained promotion from the relatively newly formed Division Four in 1959-60, but two seasons later were relegated again. It prompted Mills' decision to call time on his playing career and he was given the role of assistant trainer at the club.

Mills remained at Torquay for ten years as a coach and scout but, early in 1973, with United allegedly losing £1,000 a week, various cost-cutting measures were introduced, one of which was to scrap the reserve team which Mills had been coaching. It was the end of his long association with the club and a sad way to end.

Suddenly out of football for the first time in his adult life, Mills took a job as a traffic warden in Torquay. It was a role totally unsuited to the amiable and popular Yorkshireman, and he self-deprecatingly labelled himself 'Torquay's softest warden'.

Leaving Torquay's parking chaos behind, he took a role as warden of a home for retired teachers.

Mills passed away in 1994 but his name will forever be etched in the record books. In recent times, supporters were asked to vote for the greatest player for their club. With the voting heavily biased towards modern-day players, it is a testimony to Mills that he captured the Torquay vote. A fitting tribute to a great player and true gentleman.

Magic Moment: *Mills was given a fantastic ovation when, for one last time, he donned the No 10 shirt again in 1964 when he played in his own testimonial against Bert Head's Swindon side.*

Worst Nightmare: *With Torquay needing to win their final game of the season at Crystal Palace to clinch the 1956-57 Third Division title, Mills was brought back into the side having missed the previous game through injury. It soon became clear he was not fully fit and United could only muster a draw and lose out to Ipswich.*

TORQUAY RECORD	Appearances	Goals
League	342	81
FA Cup	23	2
League Cup	2	1

No 10. **TOMMY NORTHCOTT**

Debut: v Northampton, 30 April 1949
Farewell: v Darlington 21 May 1966

Given United's perennial struggles, both on the pitch and financially, it is remarkable how many free-scoring centre-forwards they have had on their books over the years. Thomas Theodore Northcott certainly comes under that category – a definite case of local boy made good.

Northcott was born in the Barton area of Torquay on 5 December 1931 and attended Homelands School. He began his footballing days with local side, Hele Spurs. After catching the eye as a youngster, he joined Torquay on his seventeenth birthday, with manager John McNeil pronouncing that 'the lad has moments of genius'. Northcott initially signed as an amateur and represented Devon.

Little did the six and a half thousand present at Plainmoor, who saw Northcott make his debut in the No 11 shirt for the penultimate game of the 1948-49 season, know they were witnessing the start of a prolific footballing career but there was clearly something special about the young man.

It would be another two and a half seasons, however, before Northcott established himself in the first team for any length of time and even then his record of six goals in 34 league games was not that impressive, although he had primarily been a winger in his younger days. At this time, he was also doing his National Service, as well as completing his apprenticeship as a plumber. An early pen picture revealed his hobbies as dancing ('it's good for your footwork') and snooker.

Although he formed a brief, reasonably successful forward partnership with Sammy Collins, he was always the underdog and in October

1952 was allowed to leave for Cardiff. United had formed a close arrangement with the Welsh side, which gave the Bluebirds first option on any
United player in exchange for regular loan deals. United received tough-
tackling defender Norman Parfitt and a skilful wing-half in Griff
Norman, plus a cash adjustment. Many supporters were upset to see the
local boy leave, believing he would eventually prove the natural successor
to Collins.

Cardiff were, at that time, a mid-table First Division side, mixing it
with the giants of the English game of that era – Wolves, Arsenal; and
Preston. Northcott was never prolific but nevertheless acquitted himself
well and in three seasons as a Cardiff player scored thirteen times in 71
league appearances.

The 1954-55 season saw City narrowly avoid relegation, prompting a
change of playing personnel, Tommy amongst them. In July 1955, he
joined Second Division Lincoln for a fee of £3,000, a ready made
replacement for striker Andy Graver, who had signed for Stoke.

Tommy was an instant success at Sincil Bank, scoring twenty goals in
his first season and notching 34 goals in 94 Imps appearances.

Northcott still yearned for a return to his West Country roots and,
with a move imminent, both Plymouth and Exeter showed strong interest in signing him, but there was only one place he wanted to go and, in
November 1957, Torquay manager Eric Webber got his man for a fee of
£5,000.

Webber had been desperate to sign a centre-forward, a position he
had struggled to fill adequately since the start of the season. Sammy
Collins was in the twilight of his career and Webber had even briefly
experimented with defender Colin Bettany in the No 9 shirt.

Tommy was joined in the Torquay line up by his younger brother,
George, who had begun to establish himself as first choice centre-half.
Tommy's experiences playing in a higher standard of football had
inevitably made him a better player than the one that had left Plainmoor
previously, and he quickly took over Collins' mantle as the destroyer in
chief. His thirteen goals in that return season made him the club's leading scorer and was heavily responsible for them avoiding re-election.

Northcott's best season was 1960-61. It was United's first season in
the new style Division Three, and he scored 28 league and cup goals,
including three hat-tricks.

He was an intelligent player, able to read situations and anticipate well,
often stealing a march on his slower-witted opponents. He was not particularly tall, and stockily built, but could leap well. He was a quiet and
gentle man off the field, which masked a fierce determination to succeed.

That winning mentality also meant he could look after himself if the need arose.

Northcott's career revived again with the arrival of fellow striker Robin Stubbs. The duo seemed to hit it off immediately, and soon became the most feared partnership in their division. In the three seasons they played together, they notched over 100 goals between them.

On his release from United at the end of the 1965-66 season, Northcott joined Bridgwater Town, helping them to gain the Western League championship in 1968. He also played for Barnstaple before returning to play local football in the Torquay area into his 40s.

Away from soccer, he put his apprenticeship to good use by running his own plumbing and central heating business in Torquay.

Tragically, in later life Tommy suffered from Alzheimer's disease, an affliction which sadly claims the lives of too many footballers of his era. He passed away in late September 2008. His funeral at Torquay crematorium was marked with a fitting tribute of prolonged applause from the packed congregation, who included many of his former managers and team-mates, including Stubbs, who described him as the best forward he had played with.

One of Tommy's three daughters married Peter Darke, who also played for Torquay in the late 1970s.

Magic Moment: *Northcott was selected for the England junior side on two occasions, winning caps against Scotland and Wales.*

Worst Nightmare: *Although 35 years old, Northcott, and the fans, were shocked when he was told he was being released by manager Frank O'Farrell, despite having just helped United to promotion.*

TORQUAY RECORD	Appearances	Goals
League	410	136
FA Cup	25	13
League Cup	8	1

Leading marksman Sammy Collins scores in Torquay's 5-2 home win
over Northampton in November 1954

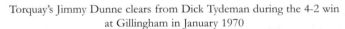

Torquay's Jimmy Dunne clears from Dick Tydeman during the 4-2 win
at Gillingham in January 1970

Ron Shaw scores Torquay's third goal in the snow at home to Brighton, December 1950

Sammy Collins aims for goal in Torquay's 1-1 home draw with Crystal Palace in August 1955. Watching is Harold Dobbie, who scored that day

Mike Green was appointed
Torquay's player-manager
in March 1977

Torquay's evergreen midfield dynamo,
family man, and author, Chris Hargreaves

Torquay F.C.

Back: John Benson, Terry Adlington, Trevor Wolstenholme, Colin Bettany, Alan Smith.
Front: Peter Anderson, John Brewster, Robin Stubbs, Tommy Northcott, Ernie Pym

On 5 November 1949 Torquay were at home to Bristol Rovers.
As centre-half Bert Head cleared the ball, it burst.
This photograph shows the inside detaching from the outer covering

Tommy Northcott and Robin Stubbs in action against Tranmere Rovers in March 1965

Ron Shaw sends in yet another typical right-wing cross

Centre-half Dick Edwards (centre) was a local hit with a band 'Quite a Bit, a Lot'

Goalkeeper Mike Mahoney comes a cropper against advertising hoardings while playing indoor soccer in the United States

Line ups for Terry Adlington's testimonial, 10 May 1966

SOUTH DEVON SELECTED XI

Colours: Gold and Royal Blue

McGUIRE

2 BOOK (P.A.)   3 BOND

5 NEWMAN (P.A.)

4 BENSON   6 WILLIAMS (P.A.)

8 SPRATT   10 STUBBS

7 JONES (P.A.)   9 BICKLE (P.A.)   11 CLARKE

Referee — M. W. BENNEY, Torquay

Linesmen:
B. DUNFORD, Paignton   (Yellow Flag)
E. E. PROWSE, Newton Abbot (Red Flag)

11 ARMSTRONG   9 SAMMELS   7 SKIRTON

10 EASTHAM   8 RADFORD

6 URE   4 McLINTOCK

5 NEIL

3 STOREY   2 McCULLOUGH

FURNELL

ARSENAL

A WORD FROM ERIC WEBBER - (Manager 1951 - 1965):

Whilst playing for Southampton, I recall having no particular ambitions towards any managerial position, and it was in fact an old Torquay player who first suggested the move.

Sid Cann, then manager of Southampton, had decided that I didn't fit in with his plans and introduced me to the Torquay United Vice-Chairman Phil Read - Chairman George Gillin was holidaying abroad at the time. After some discussion I agreed to take on the appointment - not really knowing quite what to expect, or what was expected of me.

After having some time to assess the playing-staff, it soon became obvious that confidence was sadly lacking amongst the players - both individually and in the dressing-room as a whole. It was not really surprising, because the club was being run more like a part-time outfit, and any professional approach on or off the field was virtually non-existent.

The major task was obviously to restore confidence in the players and start to build a side that would stop conceding goals and play to a pattern that would enable them to exploit their own skills - for at that level there were a lot of good players on the books. Another vital task was to change the outlook at the club - where merely avoiding re-election was seen as a success! However, results began to come and we finished in a comfortable mid-table position.

The transfer of Tommy Northcott to Cardiff City in October 1952 caused much local discussion, and in fairness most of it was adverse criticism. At that time, Chairman George Gillin was very friendly with the Cardiff City Chairman, Sir Herbert Merritt, and I knew that a great many of the local fans felt that we were at the beck and call of Cardiff City. Not so! For me there were three guiding factors: 1) that if any deals concerned exchange of players, I had to be satisfied that any incoming players would add to the playing strength, 2) that I should be satisfied about any valuation of such transfers, and 3) that I would never stand in the way of any young prospect who had a chance to make good at the top level.

In October 1953, Harold Dobbie joined the club from Plymouth in exchange for Ernie Edds. At the same time, promising young players were coming onto the playing-staff - Graham Bond, Harry Smith, Norman Lloyd - and I began to feel that we were beginning to settle and achieve the sort of consistency that could see us make a strong promotion challenge. This feeling of optimism was endorsed by some of our performances in the FA Cup - beating Leeds United 4-0, and drawing First Division Huddersfield. I remember one ardent fan saying to me "Eric, I've lived for the day that we would see a First Division side at Plainmoor - and now it's happened!"

Floodlighting was becoming a necessity, and although I chuckle to myself now at the thought of our first installation, we had floodlights as early as most of the clubs at our level. The formation of the 'A' Team was a major development, as it gave the club scope to develop local talent, and the floodlights provided a great boost as training could now be conducted

Following his dismissal as Torquay manager in 1965, Eric Webber wrote a 16-page handwritten account of his time with the club. Here is part of the transcript

Tommy Northcott and goalkeeper Colin Tinsley lie injured during Torquay's 2-0 home win over Luton in September 1965

No 11. **ERIC WEBBER**

Debut: v Leyton Orient, 27 October 1951
Farewell: v Swindon, 30 April 1955

It could be argued that based on his playing career alone, Eric Victor Webber does not warrant a place among Torquay's finest. That is not to demean his performances as a robust centre-half, but others probably have a better claim. His overall contribution to the club could not be ignored, however, as we shall see.

Webber was born at Shoreham in West Sussex on 22 December 1919, but his family moved to Fareham in Hampshire when Eric was a child, and he played his early football at Fareham Senior School. He was proficient enough to play for Fareham Town and later, Gosport Borough, where he caught the eye of Southampton's local talent spotter, and he signed for the Saints in 1938.

Initially, he played for Southampton's nursery side in the Hampshire League, but swiftly elevated himself through the ranks at the Dell, signing a professional contract in March 1939 and making his first-team debut a few weeks later.

That proved to be Webber's only first-team appearance before the war disrupted football. Eric joined the RAF but found time to guest for both Mansfield and Derby in wartime games.

As soon as hostilities had ceased, Webber returned to the Dell and immediately made the centre-half spot his own. He rarely missed a game and for two seasons was an ever present. It was, however, a frustrating time for the Saints. For two consecutive seasons, they finished third, missing promotion to the First Division by one place, on the second occasion by goal-difference (0.06 of a goal!) to Sheffield United.

He made 192 appearances for the Saints, but in October 1951 he was appointed player-manager of Torquay.

Upon his arrival at Plainmoor, he was faced with many challenges, not least the fact that the team were propping up the League, having won just two of their first sixteen games. Morale within the club was at an all-time low and the previous incumbent of the manager's chair, Alex Massie, had left after a disagreement with the directors over a number of club policies. The manager of Torquay United held few long-term prospects – Webber was the fourth in eighteen months.

Webber immediately installed himself in the No 5 shirt and quickly added to some stability to a previously nervy defence. At over 6ft tall and well built, he was an imposing figure and an uncompromising defender.

There was an immediate improvement in results, including a first ever league win over Plymouth and a 5-1 Boxing Day victory over Exeter to avenge a 4-0 defeat suffered 24 hours earlier.

The upturn in form was due to Webber installing belief in his players, ably demonstrated by a club record 9-0 win over Swindon. United lost just one of their final twelve matches and finished the season in a respectable eleventh position.

The following year followed a similar pattern – an indifferent start followed by a strong finish, thanks largely to Webber's masterstroke in securing Don Mills' return to Plainmoor.

It was at this time that Webber began the process of turning the club into a more professional outfit. He masterminded the formation of an 'A' team to compete locally and provide a stepping stone for young local talent. The team later spurned players as George Northcott and keeper Peter Wakeham, who went on to success with Sunderland and Charlton.

At the end of the 1954-55 season, Webber called time on his playing career to concentrate on his managerial duties. Whilst the club had not progressed football-wise as he had wanted, off the field there was much more of a 'feelgood' factor. Floodlights were installed at Plainmoor, not as powerful as their modern-day equivalents, but it at least allowed a number of floodlit friendlies to be played, all of which helped to swell the Plainmoor coffers.

Another major change introduced by Webber was a change of club colours. Since their formation, United had played in black and white and were appropriately nicknamed 'the Magpies'. Webber introduced the blue and gold concept to the club, feeling it was more in keeping with the town's image of sun and sand. It would be several years later that the new nickname 'The Gulls' was adopted.

After years of mediocrity, United found themselves on the verge of success when Webber masterminded a promotion challenge in the 1956-57 season. The chase went down to the wire. Everything depended on the final games of the season, but the situation was not without controversy.

If United won their game at Crystal Palace, Ipswich could not win the title. Both sides played their final games on the evening of 1 May but Ipswich's game at Southampton kicked off fifteen minutes earlier. United were drawing at Palace when news filtered through that Ipswich had won. United pressed for a winner but it was not to be. There was also discontent in the Torquay ranks that Southampton had fielded a notably under-strength side. Webber had been foiled by his former team.

Webber's tenure almost came to an end towards the closing weeks of the 1958-59 season. He had failed to build on the promotion push and two less than impressive seasons had followed. In the closing weeks of the season he was given notice of his dismissal, prompting him to unsuccessfully apply for the vacant manager's post at Chester. But in a bizarre turn of events, the Torquay board decided that the applicants to succeed Webber were not of the standard they were looking for and promptly offered him a new contract. Webber, deciding that he did not wish to uproot his family, accepted the offer. It was one of football's stranger votes of confidence.

Eric began to rebuild the side, making a number of new signings and within twelve months had secured the club's first promotion by finishing third in Division Four. He had turned Plainmoor into a fortress, losing just three home games. There was also other success, with both the reserves and the 'A' team winning the league and cup doubles at their respective levels.

Two seasons later, United found themselves back in Division Four and despite Webber's best efforts they remained stranded there. This lack of progress ultimately cost Webber his job and on 3 May 1965 he was dismissed. It was a sad way to end such a long association with the club. He had overseen many changes and signed some of the best players the club had ever possessed – Geoff Cox, Colin Bettany, John Benson and most notably, Robin Stubbs. He had dragged the club by its bootstraps and made them into a respectable and well-run league club and would be fondly remembered.

After his dismissal, which he described as 'the saddest day of my life', he took the manager's job at Poole Town, where he remained for five years before leaving the game to run the Manor House public house at Woolston near Southampton, where he remained until his retirement.

Eric had open-heart surgery in 1979 but he recovered his health to enjoy his retirement, until his passing at Southampton on 10 December 1996.

Magic Moment: *One of Webber's greatest tactical triumphs came when he saw his United side draw 3-3 with a star-studded Spurs line up in an FA Cup third round tie in January 1965. Webber had instilled the need for his players to chase everything for 90 minutes, disrupting the visitors' flowing football.*

Worst Nightmare: *Despite Webber's sterling service to the club, he was inexplicably omitted from the invitations sent to former players to attend United's first ever Wembley appearance in the 1989 Sherpa Van Trophy final.*

TORQUAY RECORD	Appearances	Goals
League	149	2
FA Cup	10	1

No 12. **ERNIE PYM**

Debut: v Millwall, 12 October 1957
Farewell: v Wrexham, 28 April 1965

Ernest Frederick Pym was another of the local players who gave Torquay valiant service over almost a decade.

Pym was born in Torquay on 23 March 1935, one of a family of thirteen. He played for various teams locally and it was manager Eric Webber, always one to give local talent an opportunity, who spotted Pym playing for St Marychurch Spurs, only a stone's throw away from Plainmoor.

He signed Ernie as an amateur at age seventeen, but Pym had to wait five years before signing a professional contract after learning his trade with the reserves and 'A' team.

Once he was given his chance, he seemed to find the transition to league football relatively easy, scoring on his debut and in his next match as well, although both games ended in defeat.

From then on, for a period of seven and a half years, Pym took up residence in the No 11 shirt, with the occasional foray into the right-wing position. He was hugely popular with the Torquay faithful, due to his never say die attitude, willingness to give his all in every game, and not one to ever shirk a tackle. He could play a bit as well. The blond receding hairline would hug the touchline, tormenting full-backs. He was a traditional-type winger – small, fast, direct and able to beat a man easily with a subtle drop of the shoulder. He laid on numerous chances and a succession of Torquay centre-forwards, Tommy Northcott in particular, were grateful for the service he provided.

He also had an eye for goal, often cutting inside to try his luck. His record of almost a goal in every three games is indeed impressive and his tally included four hat-tricks during his Torquay career.

Pym had played a pivotal role in the promotion season of 1959-60, scoring eleven goals, but ironically, his personal best season was in 1961-62 when Torquay suffered relegation from Division Three. He played in every game and scored 21 times to make United's top scorer for the season. It was a disappointing campaign, given that former England winger, Gordon Astall had joined the club. His wing partnership with Pym looked to be an exciting one, but Astall's time at Plainmoor was bedevilled by injuries which eventually forced his retirement.

It is mystifying why Pym's skills were not snapped up by a higher-division club. He was watched by various big name clubs and was the subject of transfer speculation on numerous occasions, but somehow a deal was never forthcoming. Not that it bothered Pym. He was content to serve his home-town club.

After the dismissal of Eric Webber at the end of the 1964-65 season, a number of popular players also came to the end of the line, Pym among them. He was only 30 but new manager Frank O'Farrell was his own man.

Pym teamed up again with Webber at Poole Town, remaining there for three years before returning west to join Bridgwater Town, alongside Tommy Northcott. The duo, despite their advancing years, were far too good for Western League defences and Bridgwater stormed to the league championship title in 1968.

After retiring from the game, Ernie became a builder and then a milkman before being employed for many years as the bar manager at Stover Golf Club, near Newton Abbot, where he was a single-figure handicap player himself, and where his former team-mate, Gordon Astall was, and still is, a member.

Ernie suffered a stroke and died in a nursing home on 22 October 2004.

Magic Moment: *In the opening game of the 1962-63 season, Pym scored a hat-trick in Torquay's 3-0 win at Exeter. And what a mixed bag it was. The first was a clearance that rebounded off him, the second was a brilliant solo effort as he ran from halfway and scored from a near impossible angle. The third was scored from close range.*

Worst Nightmare: *Just as Pym was in prime form, the big freeze of the winter of 1963 struck and United did not play a game from 21 December to early February.*

TORQUAY RECORD	Appearances	Goals
League	284	83
FA Cup	15	10
League Cup	8	1

No 13. **GEOFF COX**

Debut: v Queens Park Rangers, 14 December 1957
Farewell: v Swansea, 6 May 1967

Geoffrey Cox was one of Eric Webber's many astute signings for Torquay and gave the club excellent service for almost ten years.

Cox was born in the Stockingford district of Nuneaton on 30 November 1934 and went to school in that area. As a schoolboy he was a prolific centre-forward and was eventually selected for Nuneaton schools and Birmingham County Schools.

One of his fondest early memories was scoring against London Schools in a 2-0 win at Villa Park. Johnny Haynes was among the opposition that day. He was also selected for an England Schoolboys trial, although never made it into the side.

Cox's break into the professional game came almost by chance. A school friend, Gerald Belcher, was playing for one of Birmingham's youth teams and Cox would occasionally go along to watch. On one occasion, Belcher's side was a man short and Cox was drafted in. He impressed the watching coach and was offered a place on City's ground staff aged fifteen. Ironically, his friend was eventually released.

Cox's rise through the ranks was rapid. He was part of City's youth team that won the European Youth Cup in Switzerland, and made his first-team debut for the Blues at Luton aged just seventeen.

He established himself in the starting line up at St Andrews but his career was interrupted by a spell in the Army doing National Service. When he returned to Birmingham there was a new manager, a new board, and Cox was no longer guaranteed his place on a regular basis.

He was still in the first-team reckoning though, and was part of Birmingham's early forays into European football when they took part in the Inter Cities Fairs Cup. Cox played in the first European game in May 1956, a scoreless draw at Inter Milan, and also in a later tie when Birmingham beat Dinamo Zagreb 3-0 at home.

By now, Cox had been converted to a winger and he found himself playing second fiddle to the likes of Alex Govan and future Torquay team-mate, Gordon Astall. When Webber made a bid to sign him, Cox had to mull it over.

It was a big step down, with United languishing at the bottom of the Third Division, but eventually he signed with the promise of regular first-team football. It was only after he had signed that he found out that other clubs, particularly Coventry, wanted to sign him.

The introduction of Cox, together with Tommy Northcott, saw an upturn in United's fortunes during the second half of the season, and they at least avoided seeking re-election.

Cox became an integral part of Webber's sides. His speed and awareness borne from the excellent grounding he received at Birmingham. He enjoyed Webber's management style, allowing players to play to their strengths and express themselves. He also showed he still knew where the goal was, regularly getting into a double-figure tally for the season to complement Northcott's usual output. In December 1958 he notched a hat-trick against Chester and got another two years later in a home win over Reading.

Within two years of Cox's arrival, Torquay's fortunes had taken an upturn with promotion to Division Three. Cox would again experience promotion in 1965-66 under Frank O'Farrell. It was during this season that Cox cemented his place in Torquay history, when he became the first substitute to be used by the club when he replaced the injured Robin Stubbs at Doncaster on 2 October.

He also experienced the thrill of pitting his wits against the mighty Tottenham side when Torquay managed a 3-3 draw against the Londoners in the 1964-65 FA Cup in front of 20,000 at Plainmoor.

During the latter part of his Torquay United career, Cox helped to coach the club's youngsters. His career gradually wound down but he was brought back for the final game of the 1966-67 season for a nostalgic farewell.

His service to the club was eventually recognised when he was granted a testimonial in May 1968, when an invitation side took on West Ham with over 4,000 people turning up.

Cox remained in the game when Plymouth Argyle manager Derek Ufton asked him to assist with coaching the youth teams at Home Park. Cox also played a few games for the reserves.

He continued playing into his 40s, joining several other Torquay 'old boys' at Bridgwater. He also played for Welton Rovers in the Western League.

Cox remained in Torquay and became an estate agent in the town for many years, specialising in selling hotels and businesses. Now retired, he still lives in the town and plays bowls regularly with Astall, among others.

Magic Moment: *Cox had the thrill of seeing his son, Maurice, also play for Torquay. Cox junior ended up playing 63 league and cup games for the Gulls, scoring thirteen times, including a goal on his debut. Geoff also played for Huddersfield and now lives in Italy.*

Worst Nightmare: *Cox recalls feeling deflated after the much-anticipated original FA Cup replay against Tottenham was called off after Torquay had travelled to the capital and trained at Chelsea. The match was played a week later, with United losing 1-5.*

TORQUAY RECORD	Appearances	Goals
League	261	62
FA Cup	17	4
League Cup	8	2

No 14. **TERRY ADLINGTON**

Debut: v Exeter, 18 August 1962
Farewell: v Shrewsbury 13 November 1965

Torquay have been privileged to have some great keepers over the years, and none came braver than Terry Adlington. Sadly, his bravery ultimately cost him his League career.

Adlington was born in Blackwell on 21 November 1935. As a schoolboy, he was used as a full-back but always had a yearning to become a goalkeeper. Certainly his tall, well-built frame was suited to the position. During his early teenage years he played for Stonebroom Youth Club before joining Blackwell Colliery Welfare, the home club of his birthplace, playing in the Notts Alliance League. He soon proved himself to be a natural between the sticks and several league clubs were alerted to his potential.

One of those clubs was Stoke City. They invited him to play a trial match in their 'A' team against Derby, but it was not Stoke who signed him. Derby manager, Harry Storer liked what he saw and in December 1955, Adlington signed for County as an amateur.

Ten months later he signed professional terms although he was very much an understudy to regular custodian, Terry Webster.

Derby won the Third Division (North) Championship in 1956-57, with Adlington handed a token single appearance when he was picked for the clash with bottom of the table Crewe. He kept a clean sheet in a 4-0 win.

Webster eventually moved into non-league football but, frustratingly for Adlington, the No 1 jersey reverted to Ken Oxford, with Adlington used intermittently. The situation repeated itself again when England international Reg Matthews was brought to the Baseball Ground. Matthews was Adlington's boyhood hero and, showing admirable patience, he continued to ply his trade in the reserves, but all the while watching and learning from his more experienced colleagues.

Adlington remained at Derby until the end of the 1961-62 season. He was never a regular but chalked up 41 appearances. At Torquay, regular custodian Eddie Marsh had been released by manager Eric Webber who promptly negotiated a fee of £1,000 with the Rams to bring in Adlington as a replacement.

Webber soon christened him 'big fellah' and Adlington was given his debut in the opening game of the season, in which Ernie Pym's hat-trick destroyed Exeter. He was an ever present during that first season as United finished sixth.

The following season, Adlington's consistency again saw him as first choice, despite the fact that the experienced Geoff Barnsley was waiting in the wings. It was during this campaign that Adlington scored the one goal of his career. In a first round FA Cup-tie against non-league Barnet, Adlington suffered a wrist injury deemed too serious to allow him to continue between the sticks. With the concept of substitutes not yet introduced, Webber was forced to shuffle his pack, delegating goalkeeping duties to left-back George Allen, and condemning Adlington to a right-wing spot to keep him out of further harm. However, Adlington enjoyed his new-found freedom to the extent that he managed to score a last-minute goal – Torquay's sixth – against their downcast and well-beaten visitors.

Adlington missed the next three games, but it would be an injury in another FA Cup-tie that would have more serious ramifications for the big man.

On 13 November 1965, in a first round tie at Shrewsbury, Adlington, displaying typical bravery, dived at the feet of an onrushing opponent. He suffered a finger injury which was so serious that within weeks he was told that he would not recover sufficiently to continue his league career. Never again would the imposing figure with the boxer's jawbone be seen between the Torquay goalposts.

A testimonial was hastily arranged, with Billy Wright bringing his Arsenal team to Plainmoor to play a South Devon Selected XI, comprising the pick of Torquay and Plymouth Argyle players. Over 4,000 people came to pay their respects to a popular keeper and watch an entertaining 5-4 win for the hosts.

Eventually, Adlington's finger recovered sufficiently to allow him to consider a return to action. A non-league career looked likely, but across the Atlantic, 'soccer' was beginning to take off and players were arriving from all parts of the globe in a bid to extend waning careers and make more 'bucks' than they did at any other time of their career. Adlington saw this as a way back into the game and in 1967 he joined the Baltimore Bays, becoming their first choice and playing a major part in his side winning the Eastern Division title.

He then spent two years with Dallas Tornado in the formative years of the NASL before returning to England, where a planned playing contract with Boston United never materialised, to difficulties with his international clearance following his spell abroad.

Eventually, Adlington moved into management, spending six years at Dover before moving to Maidstone.

He passed away on 10 April 1994 at the relatively tender age of 58. Had he been alive, he would have been immensely proud to watch his grand niece, Rebecca Adlington, win two gold medals in swimming at the 2008 Beijing Olympics and become a national heroine.

Magic Moment: *Adlington had the opportunity to face another of his heroes, Jimmy Greaves, when United were drawn against Spurs in the FA Cup. Following a 3-3 draw at Plainmoor, Greaves scored a hat-trick in a 5-1 replay win.*

Worst Nightmare: *Adlington's career-ending finger injury proved too serious to allow him to play even a small part in his own testimonial match.*

TORQUAY RECORD	Appearances	Goals
League	148	0
FA Cup	8	1
League Cup	6	0

No 15. **ROBIN STUBBS**

Debut: v Tranmere, 24 August 1963
Farewell: v Aldershot, 17 February 1973

In a BBC poll in 2007, Robin Stubbs was voted as the greatest Gull of all time. Few would argue with the decision. He was a prolific scorer, and Torquay fans were grateful that he remained loyal for a large part of his career when surely he would have been a great success at a higher level.

Robin Gregory Stubbs was born on 22 April 1941 in the Quinton district of Birmingham. He attended Castle Road Primary School and then Oldbury Grammar School. He scored goals for a pastime as a youngster and was selected for Birmingham Schoolboys. Unsurprisingly, he was noticed by Birmingham City and taken on by them when he was sixteen. It was a lucky break for Stubbs. He was reluctantly retaking some school exams and had to talk his parents into letting him pursue a career in football.

When he turned seventeen, he was offered a professional contract and made his Birmingham debut in February 1959. In his second game he scored twice in a 7-1 win over Nottingham Forest, a side to which City had lost 0-5 in the FA Cup a few weeks earlier. In only his fourth game he went one better, nabbing a hat-trick against Leicester, and ended that first season with an impressive nine goals from just twelve games.

After such a stupendous start, his second season was something of an anti-climax as he managed to score just three times. Thereafter, he was never a regular in the side and eventually had a disagreement with Blues manager Gil Merrick, prompting a request to move elsewhere, having netted twenty times in 70 appearances.

City and Torquay had forged strong links through a connection with the directors. Stubbs was invited to go to Torquay for discussions. It was the geographical area as much as anything that made his mind up. He was put up in the Palm Court Hotel, and Stubbs had always enjoyed beach holidays. Overlooking the sunlit bay in Torquay was a far cry from Birmingham, and with the persuasion of future United chairman, Tony Boyce, he agreed to sign with the club paying out what was then a record fee of £6,000.

It soon proved to be money well spent. Stubbs was immediately handed the No 9 shirt and scored four times in his first six games. In his tenth game he scored a hat-trick against Darlington. There was even better to come. On 19 October, Stubbs scored five in a remarkable 8-3 win at home to Newport. There was an exhilarating finish to the game. With just nineteen minutes remaining, the score had only been 2-1 to Torquay. This feat remains the clubs record for the number of goals scored by one player in a match.

After Christmas, Stubbs was struck down with pleurisy and was forced to miss a month of the season. Despite this, Stubbs ended up with 25 league and cup goals. A promising sixth-place finish was attained, but United were a real Jekyll and Hyde team. At home, they were superb and scored goals for fun. They won sixteen of their 23 games at Plainmoor, scoring 60 goals. On their travels it was a completely different story. They won just four times and scored twenty goals. It was form that would cost them promotion.

Stubbs soon proved he was not a one-season wonder. He and Tommy Northcott formed the most explosive partnership in the lower divisions. Stubbs scored a remarkable 39 league and cup goals in just 44 games. He took a particular dislike to Aldershot, scoring four against them at home and a hat-trick away. He missed nine games through injury and would surely have beaten Sammy Collins' scoring record of 42 in a season had he stayed fit.

If evidence were needed that Stubbs could hold his own against better class opposition, it surely came in the FA Cup-tie with Spurs at Plainmoor in January 1965. United took a shock lead when Stubbs was brought down by a certain Cyril Knowles, later to be a United manager, and Bill Atkinson deposited the resultant penalty. Spurs hit back with three goals to seemingly kill the tie, but Stubbs had not given up and scored two late goals to give the Gulls a money-spinning replay at White Hart Lane.

Tall and upright, there was nothing complicated about Stubbs's game. He was simply a goal machine. He was strong in the air and on the ground. His game was built around scoring goals. Modern-day managers would probably decry his lack of workrate, but no one was complaining at a centre-forward who could put away a half-chance like he could. He had a suspect temperament at times, but this was often understandable given the punishment meted out to him by burly and uncompromising centre-halves. They had to try and stop him one way or another.

By now, several clubs were sniffing around Torquay's star player. He was close to signing for Blackpool for £25,000 but Stubbs decided he did not want to move. He was in the form of his life, a hero in Torquay and he enjoyed the adulation of the Torquay fans.

The 1965-66 season saw a colleague have the temerity to outscore Stubbs. The 'culprit' was new-boy Tommy Spratt, signed from Weymouth. Spratt scored eighteen, one more than Stubbs (who scored two more hat-tricks) and another dominant home record, allied to an improvement away from home, saw promotion to Division Three attained.

The step up to a higher division made no difference to Stubbs. By the end of September he had already found the net on ten occasions, including four in a 5-2 drubbing of Walsall.

As Stubbs himself admits, his poorest season, in terms of goals scored came in 1967-68. He managed just nine league goals in an injury-interrupted season and United narrowly missed out on promotion.

At the end of the 1968-69 season, United fans were distraught. Alan Brown had taken over as manager mid-season from Frank O'Farrell and wanted to bring in players. Several favourites left but the hardest pill to swallow was the departure of Stubbs in a £12,000 move to divisional rivals Bristol Rovers. As Stubbs admits, it was more down to timing then anything else. He was happy at Torquay but his marriage (to Anthea Redfern, the future *Generation Game* hostess) had ended and he felt it was the opportunity to make a fresh start. His decision to go was a spur of the moment thing.

Stubbs enjoyed his time at Rovers. He was the top scorer in his first two seasons and manager Bill Dodgin liked to play an attacking game, which suited Stubbs.

During his latter days at Eastville, Stubbs began to suffer knee cartilage problems. The treatment for such an injury was not as sophisticated as it is today and Stubbs battled on, knowing that his ailment was gradually worsening.

In January 1972, Stubbs made a welcome return to Plainmoor. United were in deep relegation trouble and had an abysmal scoring record. Manager Jack Edwards saw Stubbs as the returning messiah and the answer to his problems. The fans were drooling at the prospect of their hero saving them from the drop. The reality was very different. Stubbs's knee was continuing to trouble him. He told Torquay that he was injured but the transfer went through. As Stubbs says: 'I was playing on one leg but they watched me and thought I was doing OK so they signed me.'

Well, Stubbs didn't save them and failed to score in ten appearances. He started the following season and then missed almost four months. In reality, an operation was needed. He played just four more games before deciding to call it a day. It was a dreadful way to finish such a stellar career.

Stubbs was offered the opportunity to play in the USA but declined. The injury had taken its toll and Stubbs was slightly disenchanted with the game. There would be no non-league or coaching. He turned his back on the game.

After football, Stubbs spent many years in sales jobs. He still lives in Torquay and attends matches at Plainmoor, as well as revisiting Birmingham on occasions. These days he is involved in a part-time role as a youth worker.

Magic Moment: *Stubbs made his Wembley debut at the age of 48, when he was invited to take part in a veterans match prior to the 1989 Sherpa Van Trophy final.*

Worst Nightmare: *There was little festive goodwill on show when, on Boxing Day 1963, Stubbs was sent off after a punch up with Oxford United's 'Big' Ron Atkinson, later to become a famous manager. Atkinson was also dismissed, and later admitted that he was entirely at fault.*

TORQUAY RECORD	Appearances	Goals
League	238	121
FA Cup	12	8
League Cup	13	4

No 16. **JOHN BENSON**

Debut: v Bradford City, 22 August 1964
Farewell: v Brighton, 16 October 1970

John Harvey Benson is one of a number of former Torquay players who have gone on to management and spent a lifetime in the game.

Born in Arbroath, Scotland on 23 December 1942, Benson began his football career in the North West of England at Stockport Boys. As a wing-half he was taken on by Manchester City, turning professional in July 1961 on a wage of twelve pounds per week.

Benson played 44 league games for City in three years at Maine Road but, in the summer of 1964, joined Torquay, one of seven new signings made by manager Eric Webber in an attempt to better the sixth-place finish of the previous Fourth Division season.

Benson was put straight into the side for the opening game of the 1964-65 season at right-half and soon proved to be the pick of the new boys. His experience of top-flight football quickly came to the fore and his tireless non-stop running and workrate set an example to his teammates. He was a clever player, able to break up opposing attacks and set up chances for his colleagues in equal measure.

Benson rarely missed a game. He was unspectacular, rarely getting on the scoresheet but an important cog in the side.

Midway through the 1965-66 season, John Bond joined Torquay from West Ham. He and Benson became good friends and, as we shall see, the duo linked up on a number of occasions during their long careers in the game.

When Frank O'Farrell took over as manager, he brought some progressive new ideas to Plainmoor. In due course he introduced the 'sweeper' role and identified Benson, with his ability to read the game, as the ideal candidate to fill the role. He also made him captain.

With promotion from Division Four achieved in O'Farrell's first season, the side continued to enjoy a successful period, flirting with promotion to the Second Division but narrowly missing out, particularly in 1967-68, when they finished fourth. Benson missed the early part of that season through injury, not returning until mid-October.

Bond eventually departed, with Benson occasionally slotting into his right-back slot. Indeed, Benson played in a number of positions during his latter Plainmoor days.

By 1970, Bond was ensconced as Bournemouth manager. He had already raided Torquay to take striker Tony Scott to Dean Court, and in the October paid £12,000 to make Benson a Cherry. The fans were sorry to see him go. He had been a loyal and consistent servant and it also marked the breaking of the final link with the Webber era, something the older fans still cherished.

Benson was made captain at Bournemouth and was again a regular in the side. He made a brief return to the South West in March 1973, playing four games on loan at Exeter.

When Bond was made Norwich manager in November 1973, Benson soon followed but, in January 1975, their partnership was broken when Benson was offered the role of player-manager back at Bournemouth. The Cherries were in relegation trouble and Benson failed to save them from dropping into the Fourth Division, but he held onto his job and the next season guided them to a sixth-place finish. Unfortunately, he could not improve on those efforts and two mediocre seasons saw him replaced by Alec Stock.

Benson was quickly reunited with Bond, who was still at Norwich. Benson's playing days were now at an end but he was given the post of youth-team coach and scout at Carrow Road.

When Bond was given the manager's job at Manchester City, Benson went as well, as his assistant – a nostalgic return to his first professional club.

Bond was sacked in February 1983 and Benson given the role, but a last-day defeat at home to Luton condemned them to the drop and Benson followed Bond out of the door.

A similar scenario occurred at his next club, Burnley. Benson had again assisted Bond and again taken over as manager when his friend was dismissed, but these were difficult days at Turf Moor. The club was in turmoil, battling the drop to the Football League's bottom division for the first time, and virtually broke. Blame was apportioned to various people but Benson was, to a degree, on a hiding to nothing. Relegation preceded his inevitable sacking.

Coaching roles in Dubai and Kuwait followed. In 1990 he was appointed chief scout at Barnsley, a role he held until April 1994, when he returned to Norwich, assisting manager John Deehan with administrative duties and helping to coach the club's goalkeepers.

When Deehan went to Wigan, Benson followed as his assistant, taking over as caretaker manager in the summer of 1998, when Deehan moved to a coaching role at Sheffield United. Benson was offered the job permanently but declined, citing health problems, but he remained at the club in an advisory capacity to new boss, Ray Mathias.

These were exciting times at Wigan, with high expectations. When promotion was missed, Mathias was relieved of his duties and Benson appointed as manager. The club had, by now moved into its new JJB Stadium and seemed to be enjoying their new surroundings. Benson's side went undefeated for 26 league games and promotion seemed assured. Benson won two Manager of the Month awards but, suddenly and unexpectedly, the team's form collapsed. Wigan only made it to the play-off final, where they lost to Gillingham. Benson had the honour of leading his side out at Wembley but, days before, had announced that he was stepping down.

Benson remained at Wigan under different guises – general manager, youth development officer and director of football – before becoming assistant to Steve Bruce at Birmingham. He later became general manager at St Andrews, but in June 2006 returned to Wigan to take up a similar role, one which he remains in today.

Magic Moment: *In one of the few bright moments of his time at Burnley, Benson saw his side beat non-league Penrith 9-0 away in the FA Cup.*

Worst Nightmare: *Benson's Wigan side were 2-1 ahead with just seven minutes of extra-time remaining in the Wembley play-off final of 2000, but they conceded two goals to lost 2-3.*

TORQUAY RECORD	Appearances	Goals
League	240	7
FA Cup	12	1
League Cup	13	0

No 17. **JOHN BOND**

Debut: v Bradford City, 29 January 1966
Farewell: v Bristol Rovers, 1 February 1969

John Frederick Bond can be regarded as one of the first 'big name' signings for Torquay, having arrived at Plainmoor with a wealth of experience gained at West Ham. He continued to gain recognition after his playing days ended as a high profile, if somewhat outspoken and occasionally controversial manager of various clubs.

Bond was born in Dedham, Essex on 17 December 1932. He joined West Ham in March 1950 at the age of seventeen from Colchester Casuals, thus beginning a long association with the Upton Park club.

Within two years, Bond had made his first-team debut, having impressed in the reserves as a full-back who could also score useful goals. This scoring record did not abate once in the first team. Bond possessed a mighty kick and scored many goals from long range or from dead-ball situations. The Hammers' fans affectionately nicknamed him 'Muffin', not because of any penchant for bakery items, but after the children's TV character 'Muffin the Mule'.

Bond found success at West Ham when, in 1957-58, the Hammers won the Second Division title with Bond missing just one game and scoring eight times. He also played in the 1964 FA Cup final victory over Preston at Wembley.

This triumph saw the Hammers venture into European football the following season, gaining entry into the European Cup-Winners' Cup. Bond played four times in the early rounds but missed out on a place for the final which again, the Hammers won.

By this time, Bond was reaching the veteran stage, but he had received a superb football education at Upton Park. West Ham's style of play was greatly admired but they also possessed a nucleus of players who thought deeply about the game and it is no coincidence that Bond, along with the likes of Malcolm Allison, Frank O'Farrell and Ken Brown, would go on to become forward thinking and revolutionary coaches.

It was O'Farrell, by this time Torquay manager, who persuaded Bond to join the Gulls. Bond was now 33 and it was something of a gamble, but the arrival of a First Division player with over 400 games under his belt stirred the interest and added some experience and know-how to a squad that was looking promising promotion candidates. As part of the deal, Bond was allowed to stay in London during the week, where he continued to train with West Ham, before joining up with his new team-mates for matches.

Bond's input proved invaluable, particularly to John Benson, who had been asked to play in an unfamiliar sweeper role. Bond seemed to stroll through his games, giving a disdainful impression, but his constant encouragement and cajoling of the defence played a big part in Torquay winning promotion from Division Four at the end of that season.

Over the next two seasons, Bond missed just six games and still found the net occasionally, aided by him being the regular penalty taker. He had now settled in the town and was also thinking ahead, having opened his own sweet shop – 'Bondy's Tuck Shop' – at nearby Torre.

When O'Farrell left for Leicester, Bond applied for the vacancy at Plainmoor, but despite his vast playing experience, the board decided that he was untried as a manager and gave the job temporarily to Jack Edwards before appointing Alan Brown.

Bond drifted out of the first-team reckoning, after this and it signalled the end of his long playing career.

Clearly keen on remaining in the game, Bond accepted a coaching position at Gillingham, which preceded his first managerial appointment at Bournemouth, where he enjoyed promotion in his first season.

His success at Bournemouth led him to Norwich, where he replaced Ron Saunders. The Canaries suffered relegation from the First Division but bounced straight back and also reached the League Cup final, losing to Aston Villa.

By now, Bond was attracting press attention for some of his more flamboyant remarks. As an example, when Bradford City were twice forced to call off an FA Cup-tie due to a flu epidemic, he espoused that 'they should not be in the league if they cannot raise a team'.

In October 1980, he was appointed manager of Manchester City, who had endured a torrid start, costing Bond's former team-mate, Malcolm Allison, his job. Bond signed a number of experienced players, who turned the season around, finishing mid-table and reaching the FA Cup final before losing to a Ricky Villa-inspired Spurs.

In February 1983, Bond was sacked by City, despite their being in the top half of the table, but he was not out of the game for long, taking over at Burnley, newly relegated to Division Three. There were high expectations of an immediate promotion, and Bond brought in some of his ageing but high-earning stars from Manchester City, such as Tommy Hutchinson and Kevin Reeves to replace some of the home favourites.

Things didn't go to plan. Reeves suffered a career-ending hip injury and the side finished in mid-table. The toll on the club's finances was heavy. Bond went missing for a number of games, supposedly on scouting missions, but the Turf Moor crowd had turned against him, many blaming him for the crisis which was enveloping the club.

Bond was sacked days before the start of the 1984-85 season. It was a similar story at his next club, Swansea, who were in freefall and looking candidates to plummet through the four divisions in as many seasons. Bond again introduced experience, and released some promising youngsters, Dean Saunders included. He saved them from relegation but left in December 1985.

The managerial merry-go-round continued, with appointments at Birmingham and Shrewsbury, but Bond tasted relegation at both clubs.

Since that time, he has managed Witton Albion, scouted for Wigan, and assisted his son Kevin, who also had a successful playing career and an indifferent managerial one, as well as undertaking some media work. More recently Bond has worked as a football consultant with Northwich Victoria.

Magic Moment: *On his way to the FA Cup final with Manchester City, Bond masterminded a 6-0 fifth round win over his former club, Norwich. He celebrated by leaping from an upper tier of a stand into the players' tunnel.*

Worst Nightmare: *Such was the enduring vitriol aimed at him at Burnley, Bond was advised not to travel to Turf Moor when his Shrewsbury side was drawn to play there in the FA Cup seven years after his departure.*

TORQUAY RECORD	Appearances	Goals
League	130	12
FA Cup	7	1
League Cup	8	0

No 18. **BILL KITCHENER**

Debut: v Walsall, 17 September 1966
Farewell: v Shrewsbury, May 6 1971

Like John Bond before him, William Harry Kitchener would have connections with both West Ham and Bournemouth as well as giving fine service to Torquay.

Born in the Bedfordshire town of Arlesey on 3 November 1946, Kitchener was taken on by West Ham as an apprentice after leaving school. After playing for Bedfordshire under-16s he was spotted by the East London side. Kitchener was due to have a trial with Millwall, but the Hammers were determined to get their man and he was offered a month's trial.

He was part of their youth team that won the FA Youth Cup at the end of the 1962-63 season, and a few months later when he turned seventeen he was given his first professional contract.

The mid-1960s were exciting times at Upton Park, with the Hammers achieving an FA Cup win in 1964 and European Cup-Winners Cup success a year later. For Kitchener, a young defender, it meant that he could work at close quarters with the likes of Bobby Moore. It also meant that a first-team place was difficult to attain, with Jack Burkett a regular in Kitchener's favoured left-back slot.

With the persuasion of ex-Hammers team-mate Bond, Kitchener joined Torquay on loan in September 1966. It was United's first season in Division Three after promotion. Manager Frank O'Farrell had largely kept faith with the squad, but the early-season form had been disappointing. The euphoria of a comfortable opening-day win over Reading had quickly been forgotten after only one point was gained from the subsequent four games.

Kitchener's introduction seemed to turn the tide. His debut resulted in a 5-2 win over Walsall, with Robin Stubbs scoring four. He slotted easily into the left-back role which had been a problem position for O'Farrell. Bond had been filling the role, but it was not his favoured side.

The fans quickly took a liking to Kitchener's style. He was skilful yet aggressive with a strong left foot. Tall and upright, he was also good in the air. His years at West Ham had instilled a desire to use the ball sensibly and he liked to get forward.

His presence in the defence steadied the ship. United gradually climbed the table, a combination of Stubbs's goals and a miserly defence turning them into outsiders for promotion. It was perhaps significant that when Kitchener missed two games through injury, the Gulls lost 0-5 and 2-4.

Favourable reports on Kitchener soon found their way back to Upton Park where, despite the presence of England's World Cup winning triumvirate – Moore, Hurst and Peters – the seemingly traditional post-Christmas slump was in full swing. It prompted West Ham to recall their player and Kitchener was immediately thrust into the Hammers' first team. Again he seemed to possess the Midas touch, as the Londoners form returned. Kitchener retained his first-team slot.

The following season he found himself back in the Hammers' reserve side, as the competition for a first-team place was fierce, with several impressive youngsters vying for places. Unable to see himself breaking back into the first-team reckoning, Kitchener asked for a transfer and – despite reassurances from Hammers manager Ron Greenwood about his future – his experience of league football and big crowds meant he hoped to appear in front of more than a few hundred in reserve matches.

O'Farrell was aware that Kitchener was out of the first-team reckoning again, and pounced on the opportunity to bring him back to Plainmoor. The deal was done with Torquay paying a club record £10,000 fee, showing how highly they rated the fair-haired defender. Kitchener had little hesitation in returning, having enjoyed his previous spell.

Kitchener certainly felt at home at Plainmoor. O'Farrell had regularly raided his former team's squad, and Kitchener became the seventh ex-West Ham player on Torquay's books.

Kitchener immediately displaced Bobby Baxter in the No 3 shirt. United launched a concerted effort to gain promotion, missing out by two points after a disappointing finale, when just five points were gained from the final nine games, many of which Kitchener missed because of injury.

The name 'Kitchener' continued to appear week in, week out on the Torquay team-sheet. He was consistency personified, rarely having a bad game or allowing an opponent to get the better of him. It was difficult to believe that he was still in his early twenties. His height was also utilised at centre-half on a number of occasions, and he was equally at home in this position. When an injury crisis hit the Torquay forward line, he was also drafted in at centre-forward for a brief spell.

Whilst at Torquay, Kitchener had one eye on the future. He had begun a plumbing course whilst at West Ham and decided to continue down this route by enrolling on a course at the South Devon Technical College.

In July 1971 he was persuaded by Bond, now Bournemouth manager, to join the Torquay exodus to Dean Court. Again he joined a number of ex-Hammers, including one of his best friends from his Upton Park days, Harry Redknapp. He quickly settled at the club, with Bond adopting the same style of football as West Ham.

Sadly, Kitchener's career was to come to an abrupt end. He had noticed pains in his lower back. The club arranged for x-rays and a series of examinations. The prognosis was not good. Kitchener was told to rest but then came the devastating news that if he continued to play he risked ending up in a wheelchair. At the age of 26, Kitchener's League career was over.

He took a delivery-driving job, but was then asked if he would play part-time at Cambridge City. Feeling no ill-effects from his back, Kitchener agreed and stayed for two years before joining another ex-West Ham team-mate, Eddie Presland, who was managing Wealdstone. Presland fixed Kitchener up with a job with the London Education Service coaching in schools.

A year later, Kitchener successfully applied to join the Hampshire Police Force. He was stationed at New Milton, Ringwood, and latterly the picturesque village of Burley.

He officially retired from the force in 2001, but rejoined as a civilian and still works in a police call centre just ten minutes from his Bournemouth home.

Magic Moment: *Kitchener goals were few and far between, but he scored a beauty to set Torquay on their way to a surprise 3-1 FA Cup win over Aston Villa in November 1970.*

Worst Nightmare: *In a frustrating 1-0 defeat at Bristol Rovers in November 1966, Kitchener's header appeared to cross the line, but in any event was blatantly handled by Rovers full-back, Lindsay Parsons. Inexplicably, the referee failed to award either a goal or a penalty.*

TORQUAY RECORD	Appearances	Goals
League	167	8
FA Cup	10	1
League Cup	7	0

No 19. **JIMMY DUNNE**

Debut: v Tranmere, 19 August 1967
Farewell: v Rochdale, 9 May 1979

James Christopher Dunne is certainly one of the most colourful characters to have donned a Torquay shirt. There was never a quiet moment when 'Jimmy' was around – on or off the field. It may seen strange, therefore, that Dunne was described as 'quiet and shy' when he first came to England from his Dublin birthplace.

Dunne was born on 1 December 1947. At the age of ten he joined a boys club, Bolton Athletic, who were a highly successful junior side. Up to the age of sixteen Dunne was in a trophy-winning side each season, and the club was a great provider of talent to the more senior clubs around the Dublin area.

Dunne was in line for an Irish schoolboy cap, but in one particular match tempers flared and Dunne was sent off. The case went before a disciplinary panel, which handed Dunne a draconian six-month suspension. It cost him the chance of a cap.

Dunne left school to take up a painting and decorating apprenticeship and, his suspension served, returned to football a bit wiser. He signed amateur forms for Parkview Celtic but within half a season was signed by Irish League side, Shelbourne. In another blow to his fledgling career, Dunne was then forced to return to Parkview because of a technical irregularity with the transfer. Eventually the matter was resolved and Dunne signed a part-time professional contract.

He did not take long to make his mark and after just ten games he was signed by Millwall manager Billy Gray for £2,750 on the advice of his assistant, Bill Dodgin Jnr, who would play a further role in the Dunne career in years to come.

Within a few months, Dunne won his international cap when he was selected for the Irish Youth team against West Germany in Dublin. He waited patiently for his first-team chance at the Den, which eventually came at Easter 1967, when he made his debut against Bury. Despite Millwall winning 2-0, he was dropped for the next game and at the end of the season was released.

Disillusioned, Dunne returned to Ireland and resigned himself to taking up another decorating job. His only hope was that a coach at The Den, Jimmy Andrews, had promised to contact him if he heard of a club that was interested. Dunne didn't expect to hear anything, but Andrews soon told Dunne that Dover were interested in him as a part-timer on

£20 a week. The aforementioned Gray was, by now, manager at Notts County, and also showed interest, but Andrew was also a good friend of Torquay manager Frank O'Farrell, and tipped the United boss off about the skinny young Irishman, believing he was worth a second try.

O'Farrell took the seventeen-year-old on a pre-season trip to West Germany – the club's first ever overseas venture. United were unbeaten in four games and Dunne impressed sufficiently to be offered a contract. It was here that the Torquay players caught a glimpse of the real Jimmy Dunne. The players were sharing rooms in a hotel and apparently Dunne had a habit of sleeping with his mouth wide open. His room-mate, John Smith, caught an errant moth and Dunne's wide-open mouth was too good an opportunity to miss. The moth was duly spat out at some speed, followed by a string of Irish expletives!

O'Farrell had no hesitation in throwing Dunne into the line up for the opening game of the 1978-68 season, at left-half. Dunne must have thought that league football was easy. United were unbeaten in their first ten games.

Dunne turned in a string of impressive performances and missed just four games in that first season. He visibly grew in confidence and the wicked sense of humour soon came to the fore making him a popular fig-ure both on and off the field. The team photos of that era display the difference. In his first photo, Dunne is seen in the back row, head down and unsmiling. A year later, he is in the front row, grinning wickedly and with the short back and sides replaced by a thick mane of black hair. The droopy moustache followed a while later. Thanks to a strict training regime, he became physically stronger.

Dunne adopted a cavalier to his football and, indeed, his life. Occasionally he was indisciplined, irking officials and opposing support-ers alike, but it always seemed mischievous rather than malicious, and was part of his endearing character.

He remained an integral part of the Torquay side, equally at home at half-back or centre-half. He was also strong in the air, an excellent pass-er and scored some useful goals. He was called into the 22-man Republic of Ireland squad for the 1970 World Cup preliminaries, although he did not get the call.

It seemed inevitable that a higher standard of football beckoned, and indeed it did when Bill Dodgin, now manager at Fulham, paid £17,000 to take him to Craven Cottage in the summer of 1970. Dunne settled into the Cottagers' side, a mix of bright young talent and vastly experienced stars such as Bobby Moore and Alan Mullery. It was a successful season for Dunne. Fulham finished as runners up in Division Three and on 30

May 1971, he was selected for the full Republic of Ireland side against Austria in Dublin. It proved to be Dunne's only cap, and it was not the night he would have wished, as his outstretched leg diverted the ball past his own keeper, Alan Kelly in a 1-4 defeat.

Dunne remained at Fulham for four seasons before embarking on a brief spell in South Africa with Durban City. However, he hankered after a return to League football and he returned to Fulham.

His second spell there was not so happy, and when Torquay manager Malcolm Musgrove offered him the opportunity to return to Plainmoor in April 1976, Dunne jumped at it. A fee of £5,000 sealed the deal as he arrived in time to play in the final game of that season.

Dunne was happy back amongst familiar faces and he quickly reminded the United faithful of what they had missed, mixing the occasional madcap moment with some great football and astute passing.

In May 1979, he was granted a testimonial when his All Stars team containing Moore and Mullery, as well as the likes of Jimmy Greaves, took on Bristol City. Under league rules at the time, Dunne had not served the ten years required to be granted a testimonial, and he was forced to retire at the age of 31. Many believed he had a few good years left in him.

After leaving League football, he played briefly for Minehead before embarking on two separate spells in Australia with Green Gully and Brisbane City. He also made a cameo appearance back in Ireland for Limerick United.

He is still fondly remembered at Plainmoor as someone who played football with a smile on his face.

Magic Moment: *Dunne headed home two goals in the last ten minutes to clinch a thrilling 2-1 victory over Scunthorpe in April 1968. However, a thick fog had enveloped Plainmoor and few of the 10,000 crowd knew what had happened.*

Worst Nightmare: *Whilst playing for Fulham at Sunderland, Dunne pulled down his shorts in front of a section of the Roker Park crowd. After a complaint, he was taken to court and fined.*

TORQUAY RECORD	Appearances	Goals
League	248	18
FA Cup	11	0
League Cup	15	1

No 20. **ALAN WELSH**

Debut: v Mansfield, 18 November 1967
Farewell: v Notts County, 3 May 1972

Alan Welsh is perhaps one of the most underrated United players but, as his scoring record suggests, he was a top-notch striker and highly skilful player.

Born on 9 July 1947 in Edinburgh, Welsh was relatively inexperienced when Torquay manager Frank O'Farrell signed him in November 1967 for £5,000, having played, in two years, just five first-team games for Millwall, who brought him south in July 1965 from Scottish side Bonnyrigg Rose.

O'Farrell had been pondering the make-up of his strike-force for some time. The side had started the season well but then hit a poor run of form in October, losing three out of four, including a 0-5 defeat at Bury and a 1-5 loss at Shrewsbury in the space of a week. Those defeats marked the end for out-of-sorts keeper John Dunn and centre-forward, Jim Fryatt, he of the 'mutton chop' sideburns. Star striker Robin Stubbs was an automatic choice, but Fryatt was too similar in style. O'Farrell also had Fred Binney and Doug Clarke at his disposal, but decided that the small, darting Welsh was the type of player he wanted.

Welsh soon showed why the astute O'Farrell had signed him. He was tricky, mobile and displayed great ball skills. Stubbs missed a number of games through injury, which regularly interrupted attempts to form a decent partnership with Welsh, but it didn't bother the Scotsman, who began to score a few goals with only a disappointing run in preventing promotion.

Welsh, sharing digs with Irishman Jimmy Dunne, began the new season with a niggling injury that kept him out of the side. He was on the bench for the most anticipated game of the season so far, the local derby against Plymouth at Home Park. Argyle boss Billy Bingham upped the ante by making some remarks to the press, claiming United were a lucky side. It may not be up to the José Mourinho class of psychological warfare, but it was enough to fire the United players up. In the second half Welsh was sent on and proceeded to collect a superb pass from Stubbs to fire a shot past Pat Dunne and give United their first ever victory at Plymouth.

When O'Farrell departed to take over at Leicester, he was keen to take both Ken Sandercock and Welsh with him, but whilst Sandercock eventually moved, Torquay refused all offers for Welsh.

Welsh admits that he did not see eye to eye with new manager Alan Brown, and found himself languishing the reserves for long periods. When he did return to favour, he soon made up for lost time, scoring four times in three games on his comeback.

He maintained his form, finishing as United's leading scorer with fifteen and showed that he was equally at home in a midfield role or playing out wide. Scotsman Welsh had been joined in the Torquay squad by another Welsh – Eric – who to add to the confusion was a Northern Irish international.

Welsh (Alan) again finished as United's top scorer in the 1971-72 season, scoring fourteen times, including a hat-trick in a second round FA Cup-tie against non-league Barnet. His goals could not prevent the Gulls from being relegated from Division Three, however, and that summer he was signed by Plymouth manager Ellis Stuttard for £15,000.

Welsh soon made his mark at Home Park, scoring once in his third game and twice in his fourth. He enjoyed playing in front of larger crowds than he had been used to, particularly at Elland Road, when Argyle ran the mighty Leeds close in an FA Cup fourth round tie.

Welsh finished as Argyle's top scorer with thirteen goals, and the following season hit the headlines when Argyle surprisingly reached the semi-finals of the League Cup. Welsh was particularly influential during that cup run, scoring twice in a 3-0 win at QPR and another in the fifth round win at Birmingham. Both opponents were First Division sides at the time. Argyle eventually lost to Manchester City in the two-legged semi-final, just one step from Wembley.

The second leg at Maine Road proved to be Welsh's final Argyle appearance. Given his performances, it was a surprise to Pilgrim fans when he was allowed to leave for Bournemouth. He remained at Dean Court until August 1975, when he returned to Millwall before moving again, this time to South Africa to play for Cape Town City.

Welsh settled in South Africa for ten years, playing and coaching. He eventually returned to England and Millwall, where he worked in the commercial department. He later gained employment with a printing company.

Now living in Forest Hill, London, Welsh still keeps himself fit by running and playing squash regularly.

Magic Moment: *Welsh had the pleasure of playing against Pele when Plymouth took on (and beat) the mighty Santos at Home Park in 1973.*

Worst Nightmare: *Welsh was unable to celebrate completing his hat-trick against Barnet. His third goal came about when the opposing keeper blasted the ball against a delicate part of his anatomy. The ball looped back over the keeper with Welsh collapsing to the ground in agony.*

TORQUAY RECORD	Appearances	Goals
League	145	45
FA Cup	11	4
League Cup	5	1

No 21. **MICKY CAVE**

Debut: v Southport, 10 August 1968
Farewell: v Shrewsbury, 6 May 1971

Despite a relatively short career as a Torquay player, Michael John Cave was one of the most popular players to have graced Plainmoor. Indeed, he was universally popular at all his clubs, not least for his ability to score spectacular, long-range goals.

Cave was born in Weymouth on 28 January 1949 and represented Dorset Schools. As one of the better local players, he was snapped up by Weymouth in 1966 and combined playing for his home town club while studying engineering.

Having come so close to promotion in May 1968, Torquay (and former Weymouth) manager Frank O'Farrell justifiably believed that a couple of tweaks to his line up would give him the extra few per cent needed to ensure Division Two football for the first time. With funds available, following the sale of John Smith to Swindon, he returned to his former club to sign Cave in July 1968, one of four new signings during the close season.

Cave was a debutant for the opening game of the 1968-69 season, playing at inside-left. He scored in his second home game against Barrow but initially found the faster pace of League football difficult to adjust to and was consequently in and out of the side.

Results-wise, it was a disappointing start and, in December, O'Farrell accepted the managerial position at Leicester. His successor was Alan Brown. The former Luton manager had been O'Farrell's chief rival for the Leicester job and, when he didn't get it, was promptly sacked by Luton for showing an interest.

The new manager made Cave a regular in the side, liking his strong-running style. Cave with his tousled hair and droopy Mexican style moustache, almost a fashion must-have for a 1970s footballer, had by now adapted to the pace of the professional game. Results began to pick up but, Robin Stubbs aside, goalscoring was to prove United's nemesis. Cave's meagre tally of four made him the equal second top scorer as a sixth-place finish was attained.

The following campaign saw United without Stubbs, transferred to Bristol Rovers, but the lack of their talismanic leader did not seem to affect the team early on. The forwards were in free-scoring mood, with Cave making useful contributions, particularly at Bournemouth, where he scored twice. Cave's efforts were usually spectacular, but a devastating six-goal Boxing Day defeat at Home Park, Plymouth, knocked the stuffing out of the side, and form and promotion hopes faded away.

Cave spent one more season at Plainmoor before former team-mate John Bond signed him for Bournemouth for a fee of £15,000. Cave initially struggled at Dean Court and in March 1972 was briefly loaned to Plymouth.

He quickly endeared himself to the Argyle fans by scoring twice on his debut and notched four goals in his eight appearances. If the fans had their way he would have become a Pilgrim permanently, but he returned to Bournemouth with new-found confidence and as a better player.

In August 1974, York City paid out what was, at that time, a club record fee of £18,000 to take Cave to Bootham Crescent. City had just won promotion to Division Two and Cave quickly established himself as one of their better calibre players. Despite being relegated after two seasons, Cave was voted as York's 'Clubman of the Year' in 1975-76. He also had a taste of soccer American style, with a loan spell at Los Angeles Skyhawks.

In February 1977, after 109 games and fifteen goals, he returned for a second spell at Bournemouth for a fee of £10,000 but, having tasted the high life in the USA, he set his sights on finishing his career there. He had another loan spell, this time at Seattle Sounders, where he became a star player. The NASL was taking off big time, and the opportunity to pit your wits against the likes of Pele and Franz Beckenbauer in front of 50,000 crowds was a far cry from trotting out to luke-warm applause from 3,000 people at Bootham Crescent on a February evening.

Cave left Bournemouth in 1978, joining Seattle on a permanent basis. Among his more illustrious team-mates were Bobby Moore and Harry Redknapp. He remained a 'Sounder' until 1980, when he also played briefly for the Cleveland Cobras in the inferior American Soccer League.

In 1981 he moved again, this time to Pittsburgh Spirit, who competed in the US Major Indoor Soccer League. He continued playing and was appointed coach.

Cave had seemingly settled in the States, when tragedy struck. On 6 November 1984 his body was found at his house near Pittsburgh. Subsequent test showed that he had died of carbon monoxide poisoning. Detectives discovered his car ignition had been switched on, its fuel tank empty and the engine cold. Cave had been in good health and there was no evidence of a suicide note. A verdict of accidental death was passed at the Coroner's hearing. Cave was just 35 years old.

Magic Moment: *Cave's popularity at Bournemouth was recognised posthumously, when the club's annual Player of the Year award was named after him.*

Worst Nightmare: *Cave was part of the Torquay side which was involved in the club's first ever abandoned match at Plainmoor. In March 1971 the encounter with Shrewsbury was called off in the 63rd minute, following torrential rain which had turned the pitch into a quagmire*

TORQUAY RECORD	Appearances	Goals
League	114	17
FA Cup	8	3
League Cup	7	1

No 22. **KEN SANDERCOCK**

Debut: v Rotherham, 14 September 1968
Farewell: v Barnsley, 7 December 1974

Kenneth Leslie Sandercock was certainly one of the most talented youngsters that Torquay have produced over the years.

Sandercock was born on 31 January 1951 in Plymouth and brought up in Plymstock on the outskirts of the city. He played for Plymouth Schools and Plymstock United in the Plymouth and District League, and not surprisingly quickly came to the attention of local professional side, Plymouth Argyle.

On leaving school, Sandercock had an offer of an apprenticeship with Argyle but never signed. His parents felt it would be better if he learnt a trade. Being a footballer in the mid-1960s may have appeared to be a glamorous life, but it was not well paid, certainly as a young lower league player. And so, the young Sandercock embarked on a 'career' as a painter and decorator.

He continued to play football and it was playing for the Devon youth team that he was spotted by Torquay. United manager Frank O'Farrell immediately took a shine to the youngster and became determined to sign him. After much persuasion, Sandercock and his parents agreed that he would sign for the Plainmoor club.

O'Farrell's determination soon paid off. Sandercock's talent was obvious and, aged just seventeen, and still an apprentice, he was given his first-team opportunity. His tremendous workrate in midfield made up for his lack of inches, but initially the United fans saw little of him in action. O'Farrell used Sandercock mainly in away matches, where he felt he was better served in the defensive style of play United had adopted on their travels. At home they played a more attacking style and O'Farrell felt that the youngster had not physically developed sufficiently to fit into this more aggressive mode of play.

But Sandercock proved more and more indispensable as the season wore on. He ended up playing 34 league and cup matches and showed his versatility by also appearing as a winger and inside-forward, despite having initially joined the club as a forward.

By December 1968, O'Farrell had left to take up the reins at Leicester. Keen to strengthen his squad at Filbert Street, he soon made no secret of the fact that he would like to sign Sandercock, but the youngster clearly had a wise head on those young shoulders, declaring that, despite the opportunity to join a First Division club, he was in no hurry to leave Torquay and would only do so if the club needed the money.

O'Farrell's replacement, Alan Brown, seemed resigned to losing Sandercock. As transfer deadline-day approached, he attempted to sign ready-made replacements to allow Sandercock to go on loan to Leicester, but the deals fell through and the youngster remained at Plainmoor.

O'Farrell was not the only one wise to Sandercock's talents. Bristol City also enquired as to his availability, and Reading forward Dennis Allen was so impressed when he opposed Sandercock that he alerted his brother, the QPR manager, Les Allen.

As the 1969-70 season unfolded, O'Farrell was still in pursuit of his man. Leicester had reached the FA Cup final the previous season, losing to Manchester City, but had also been relegated to Division Two. Set on an instant return to the First Division, Sandercock was one of a number of targets. Apparently the Leicester boss made no less than six attempts at finalising a deal, with Torquay also declaring that the fee on offer was not enough.

Eventually, with several new signings on board, Brown was prepared to let Sandercock go. The versatile player had played much of the season at right-back, a problem position for Brown but the signing of the experienced Cec Smyth from Exeter filled the void. Finally, in November 1971, a deal was agreed. Torquay received £8,000 with the promise of a further £2,000 if Sandercock played fifteen first-team games, gained international honours, or was transferred to another club. Even then, Sandercock was less than excited at the prospect of joining a bigger club. He planned to get married in the New Year and had set his heart on settling in Torquay.

O'Farrell had finally got his man. Even Brown was happy for Sandercock, believing that the opportunity to play at a higher level would help him stake a claim for England Under-23 honours.

Sandercock was immediately included in the first-team squad, alongside such names as Peter Shilton, David Nish and Peter Rodrigues for the match at Blackpool. Sandercock came on as a substitute and impressed sufficiently to be given a starting role for the next game.

Sandercock made a total of ten appearances that season, five from the bench, but during the following campaign he didn't get a look in. O'Farrell had the luxury of choosing practically the same eleven week in, week out, as Leicester swept to the Second Division title as well as reaching the FA Cup quarter-finals, where they were beaten by the eventual double winners, Arsenal..

With Leicester back in the top flight and O'Farrell having been lured to Old Trafford as manager, Sandercock's chances of a regular first-team berth seemed even more remote, so the chance to rejoin Torquay on loan was heaven-sent.

By this time, Jack Edwards was in charge and the return of Sandercock in November 1971 gave the club a much-needed morale boost. Sandercock's reintroduction could not prevent United's eighth consecutive defeat, but a week later he received a great welcome back at Plainmoor as he, along with forward Dave Tearse, another signing from Leicester, played a major part in ending the poor run with a 3-1 win over Blackburn.

Sandercock's loan move was soon made permanent, although he was unable to prevent United's relegation from Division Three.

By this time, his younger brother, Phil had also broken into the Torquay side. Ken was now back in familiar territory and quickly settled into the side on a regular basis, playing in a number of different positions. Unfortunately, United fared little better back in the Fourth Division and failed to break into the top half for the next two seasons.

By the 1974-75 season, United were struggling both on the field and financially. Whilst younger brother Phil's career was on the up, Ken's was suffering through injuries. In January 1975, he had his contract cancelled, partly, no doubt, in an effort to save on wages as the whole future of the club seemed in doubt at one stage.

Sandercock briefly joined Yeovil before moving to Western Australia, where he played for exotically named Floreat Athena and then Manley Windmills.

In 1997, whilst still residing in Australia, Sandercock succumbed to cancer at the age of just 46.

Magic Moment: *Ken was proud to play alongside his younger brother Phil in the Torquay side, making them the first brothers to appear for the club.*

Worst Nightmare: *Sandercock was stretchered off only minutes into his full debut for Leicester in a match at Bolton.*

TORQUAY RECORD	Appearances	Goals
League	165	6
FA Cup	9	0
League Cup	6	0

No 23. **JOHN RUDGE**

Debut: v Bournemouth, 25 January 1969
Farewell: v Oldham, 22 January 1972

Without doubt, John Robert Rudge can be described as one of football's true gentlemen. He is better known as a long-serving and successful manager in the game, but also had a playing career in the lower leagues, and it was the Torquay fans who saw him at his best during his playing days.

Born on 21 October 1944 in Wolverhampton, 'Rudgie' attended St Joseph's Roman Catholic School in his home town and showed prowess at football, cricket and basketball.

It was football at which he really excelled. He was taken on as a schoolboy by Wolves, where he was utilised mainly as a winger.

In his early days he used to help out on the family's fruit and veg market stall. It meant early-morning starts and the daily delight of collecting a trolley from a rat-infested cellar and pushing it up a steep hill. Such an insight into 'real' life made the young Rudge even more determined to become a footballer. His evenings were spent playing football in the street, except when Wolves, with the likes of Billy Wright in the side, were at home, when Rudge would watch from the terraces, standing on an upturned orange box borrowed from the stall.

Despite the interest from Wolves, Rudge began his professional career at Huddersfield, signing for the Yorkshire club in 1962, firstly as an apprentice on £7 a week. He moved into digs previously occupied by Denis Law, who had just moved on to Manchester City.

He spent four years at Leeds Road but made only five first-team appearances. In 1966 he went to Carlisle for £7,000, where he at least tasted first-team football on a more regular basis. Under manager Alan Ashman, Rudge witnessed a passing style of play which would engender itself on Rudge's coaching style in later life.

Although being a Carlisle player was preferable to dodging rats, it was still far from a glamorous life. Rudge's wages were £27 and 10 shillings a match. Money was tight. On one occasion after a heavy away defeat, the team bus ran out of petrol on the bleak surrounds of Shap.

Rudge's time at Brunton Park was blighted by injury, a familiar theme throughout his playing career. Despite this, he would be on the move again. At the other end of the country, Alan Brown had just taken over as manager of Torquay, having succeeded the Leicester-bound Frank O'Farrell. Brown's ethos was one of attacking play, branding O'Farrell as too defensively minded, and he set about bringing in players that would suit this approach. Rudge was signed for £7,000 but was initially used in midfield rather his more familiar forward role.

Rudge was restored to the forward line for the start of the 1969-70 season and started like a train, scoring seven times in the first six games. Short in stature, Rudge relied on speed and movement and he was benefiting from the intelligent midfield guile of new signing Tommy Mitchinson, but another injury knocked him out of his stride. He still finished the season with seventeen league and cup goals to make him the club's top scorer.

Rudge was now relishing the opportunity of regular first-team action, and the following season he remained injury free. Several penalties helped him reach the twenty-goal mark, including a hat-trick against Tranmere.

The 1971-72 season was to be Rudge's last as a player at Plainmoor. By mid-season, the team had hit a terrible run of form. In an attempt to turn things around, manager Jack Edwards brought back the legendary Robin Stubbs from Bristol Rovers, with Rudge moving in the opposite direction as part of the deal.

He was part of an attractive side at Rovers, which featured the 'Smash and Grab' act of Alan Warboys and Bruce Bannister. Another move, this time to Bournemouth, followed but again injuries took their toll, to the extent that a troublesome Achilles eventually forced his retirement.

Rudge made a return to Plainmoor in 1978 when he was appointed coach by new manager Mike Green, his former captain at Rovers.

Late in 1979, Rudge was offered the number two role at Port Vale under manager John McGrath. They were desperate times at the Potteries club – deep in debt, attracting gates of just over 2,000 and facing a battle against re-election. They survived, but McGrath was eventually sacked and Rudge handed the hot seat.

The rest, as they say is history. Rudge became a living legend at Vale, staying as manager for fifteen years. He led them to three Wembley appearances, promotion to the Championship, an Anglo-Italian Cup final, not to mention developing a host of young talented players who netted over £10 million in transfer fees.

Throughout this time, Rudge remained the modest, self-effacing person he always was. That is not to say he did not possess a steely determination – anyone who survives such a long time in the perilous world of football management must possess such a trait. But he was never the rant-and-rave type manager.

His eventual departure from Vale was, however, controversial. After a poor run of form, Rudge was dismissed in January 1999. All he received was a short letter informing him of the decision. He was offered no thanks or a pay off and took the matter to an industrial tribunal, which found in his favour, awarding him £300,000 plus costs of £150,000, much less than he would have received if his contract had been paid up.

The decision to sack him outraged the Vale fans. If the chairman wanted him to go quietly, the supporters didn't. They organised a 'flat cap' march in deference to Rudge's favoured and seemingly permanently attached headwear. They also organised a celebratory dinner, when a remarkable 750 people turned up.

Not surprisingly, Rudge was not out of a job for long. He was appointed director of football at neighbours Stoke City, a position he still holds today, working alongside manager Tony Pulis, another former Bristol Rovers team-mate. After a lifetime in the game, Rudge is as enthusiastic as ever and finally experiencing top-flight football at the Britannia Stadium.

Magic Moment: *Rudge scored in a 3-1 win over top of the table Fulham in October 1970, when the* Match of the Day *cameras made a rare visit to Plainmoor.*

Worst Nightmare: *In March 1971, Rudge had a penalty saved by former Torquay keeper John Dunn. It might have given United a shock victory over Aston Villa.*

TORQUAY RECORD	Appearances	Goals
League	96	34
FA Cup	6	3
League Cup	8	3

No 24. **PHIL SANDERCOCK**

Debut: v Brighton, 29 November 1969
Farewell: v Southend, 13 May 1977

The younger brother of another United hero, Ken, Philip John Sandercock was born in Plymouth on 21 June 1953. With Ken making such an impression at Torquay from an early age, Frank O'Farrell wasted little time in persuading Sandercock junior to also sign for the Plainmoor club.

Ken rapidly gained a place in the United first team and began to earn rave reviews, but rumours began circulating that his younger brother was possibly even better.

Older supporters can debate that long and hard, but O'Farrell was certainly impressed enough, so that when regular left-back Bob Glozier was injured, he had no hesitation in drafting in Phil for a surprise debut at Brighton. Sandercock was not yet seventeen years old.

It was to be his only appearance for that season, O'Farrell keen to nurture the youngster's talent carefully, but it would be another three years before Sandercock was given anything like an extended run in the side when he played in the final ten matches of the 1972-73 season.

After that, it was rare to see a United side run out without the well-built defender in their line up. Strong and resolute, he made the left-back position his own. The 1973-74 season saw him appear in every match, as well as notching his first goal, from the penalty spot, in a 3-0 win over Doncaster.

Indeed, Sandercock became the club's regular spot-kick expert. Of his thirteen United goals, ten came from penalties. One of those, against Workington in February 1975, atoned for an earlier own-goal he had put past Gulls' keeper Mike Mahoney.

Like his brother, other clubs were alerted to the talents of Phil and, during the summer of 1977, manager Mike Green instigated a clear out of the old guard. Sandercock was allowed to leave and joined Fourth Division rivals Huddersfield.

He remained at Leeds Road until September 1979, where he was a regular in the side, making 81 league appearances and scoring once before joining Northampton. He remained with the Cobblers until 1981, racking up a further 69 appearances before leaving League football at the age of 28 to sign for Nuneaton.

Sandercock remained up country after his retirement and is now living in Milton Keynes.

Magic Moment: *When Sandercock made his debut at Brighton, he became United's youngest ever first-team player aged just sixteen years, five months. The record stood until 1993, when David Byng made his debut, aged sixteen years and 35 days.*

Worst Nightmare: *On 3 January 1977, in a home encounter with Cambridge United, Torquay centre-half Pat Kruse scored the fastest ever own-goal in Football League history, timed at six seconds. To make matters even worse, Sandercock also headed past his own keeper, Terry Lee, in the 44th minute. Ironically, Lee had not needed to make one save from a Cambridge effort. Fortunately, United fought back to draw 2-2.*

TORQUAY RECORD	Appearances	Goals
League	205	13
FA Cup	7	0
League Cup	13	0

No 25. **MAL LUCAS**

Debut: v Bristol Rovers, 18 March 1970
Farewell: v Reading, 28 February 1973

Peter Malcolm Lucas is one of only a handful of full internationals who have worn the Torquay shirt over the years, although his caps were won some seven years before joining the club.

Born in Wrexham on 7 October 1938, Lucas won Welsh schoolboy honours and looked to have a bright future in the game. He spent two seasons as a schoolboy at Bolton, but reluctantly left as he found the regular travel from his home a problem. He returned to work in the mines but also went to Liverpool for five weeks, but again the travel was burdensome and he went back to playing village football for a number of teams in North Wales.

Cyril Lea, a team-mate from one of the local sides, Bradley Rangers, had been taken on by Leyton Orient and spoke to Lucas about the possibility of going there on trial. Lucas's enthusiasm was reunited and he decided to have another attempt at breaking into the professional game.

After a successful two week trial, he was taken on as a part-timer, travelling at the weekends for matches and then returning home. Lucas was also afraid that if he signed full-time, he would be called up for National Service. It was not that he was fearful of signing up, but circumstances at home made it difficult. His father had died when Lucas was young, and he did want to leave his mother to fend for herself. Eventually, he discovered that he was exempt from call-up anyway, being classed as a dependent relative.

Eventually, he settled in London and signed for Orient, then a respectable mid-table Second Division side.

Lucas soon became a fixture in the Orient half-back line, usually in his favoured right-half position. Measuring 5ft 8ins, he was perhaps slightly too tall to be placed into the pocket dynamo category, but he was a busy, combative midfielder. He was the workhorse of the side, content to graft and win the ball for other, more creative, players. As a consequence, his goalscoring record tallies just seventeen goals in well over 450 League appearance in total. When he did score, however, they were usually spectacular, none better than his first ever league goal, a 35-yard piledriver against Middlesbrough in August 1961.

Orient found unexpected success in the 1961-62 season, when they were the shock Second Division runners up to Liverpool. They clinched promotion to the top flight on the last day of the season under manager Johnny Carey, the former Manchester United defender. They were rewarded by for their efforts by director Leslie Grade, a theatrical agent, who paid for each of the players and their wives to go on holiday to Majorca, a real luxury trip in those days.

This success brought its reward for Lucas. After gaining an Under-23 cap, he was given his full international debut by Wales in April 1962, playing in a comfortable 4-0 win over Northern Ireland. He soon gained a second cap against Mexico (losing 1-2).

Orient's spell in the big time lasted just one season. They finished well adrift at the bottom, despite memorable victories against West Ham, champions Everton, and Manchester United in the space of twelve days.

Lucas gained two more full caps, against Scotland and England in 1963, as well as going on a tour of South America. With Orient on the slide, however, and with a new manager in Benny Fenton, with whom Lucas had differing views at times, he joined Norwich in September 1964 for a fee of £16,000 plus Colin Worrell in exchange. He immediately slotted into the side and played in every remaining game of that season, captaining the team on a couple of occasions in the absence of regular skipper, Barry Butler.

Lucas became the Canaries' 'Mr Consistency', and the fans loved him for his no-nonsense approach to the game. In total, he played 204 games for the East Anglian outfit, scoring ten goals, but on transfer deadline-day in March 1970, he was snapped up on a free transfer by Torquay boss

Alan Brown. Lucas had been out of the Norwich side with an injury, but was told by then manager Ron Saunders that other clubs were looking at him, although he admits now that he was perhaps hasty in accepting United's offer rather than biding his time to consider others.

Brown saw Lucas as the perfect foil to the passing skills and creativity of fellow midfielder Tommy Mitchinson, whose clever play and strong tackling had seen him dubbed 'The Prime Minister of Plainmoor'.

United had been on a poor run since a 0-6 Boxing Day drubbing at Plymouth, and were in danger of being sucked into the relegation battle. It cannot be said that Lucas's arrival had an immediate impact. It was not until his fifth game that he enjoyed the pleasure of winning, but it was his first goal for the club that set the Gulls on their way to a morale boosting 3-0 win over Rochdale.

The 1970-71 season saw Lucas miss just three games as the campaign began promisingly, although results gradually petered away. Lucas provided one of the highlights of the season when his screaming shot was the catalyst for a Boxing Day win over Plymouth on a snow-covered Plainmoor. On Good Friday, United stunned a 17,000 crowd by also winning the return match at Home Park, to date, United's only ever league 'double' over their Devon rivals.

Lucas and his wife settled in Torquay, running a guest house in Babbacombe.

The following year saw United relegated and Lucas suffer an injury-interrupted season, firstly breaking a bone in his foot, and then suffering from appendicitis. Although approaching his mid-30s, he remained for two more seasons. He was made captain and it was easy to draw comparisons to Nobby Stiles, certainly in appearance, with Lucas sporting long sideburns, straggly hair and missing the odd tooth here and there.

Lucas admits that he had become frustrated with the standard of play and had differing views on some of the coaching methods. He decided to take up an offer from Lowestoft. United chairman Tony Boyce tried to persuade him to stay by offering him a coaching role, and also to assist him in going into the hotel trade, but Lucas's mind was made up. The offer from Lowestoft came about after the team stayed at his guest house.

Initially, Lucas played and helped to coach Lowestoft, staying in a flat there before returning back to Torquay every two weeks or so.

He later played and managed other East Anglian sides Gorleston and Hoveton. In 1998 he returned to Gorleston as assistant manager to former Norwich winger Dale Gordon.

After leaving the full-time game, Lucas went into insurance, worked for the local Electricity Board, and then worked for a leisure company.

He continues to live near Norwich and spends much of his leisure time coarse fishing.

Magic Moment: *Lucas's popularity at Norwich was such that he was inducted into the Canaries' Hall of Fame.*

Worst Nightmare: *Lucas almost didn't sign for Torquay. He and his wife travelled to Devon by train and, whilst passing along the coast line at Dawlish, huge waves engulfed their carriage. Lucas's wife was wondering what she had let herself in for.*

TORQUAY RECORD	Appearances	Goals
League	122	3
FA Cup	8	0
League Cup	5	0

No 26. **IAN TWITCHIN**

Debut: v Tranmere, 3 April 1970
Farewell: v Northampton, May 1 1981

'Twitch'. Perhaps there has never been a more inappropriate nickname for a player, because Ian Robert Twitchin was as steady and solid a player that you are ever likely to see.

Twitchin became only the fourth player to rack up 400 League appearances for Torquay, as a succession of managers realised they could not do without his cool head and commitment. Of those 400 games, only a handful would be put into the 'could have done better' category.

Born in Teignmouth on 22 January 1952, Twitchin is the classic case of local boy made good. He was a United supporter as a youngster and like most boys of that age had ambitions to become a professional footballer although, realising that the road to that ambition could be a long and tough one, he was prepared to study to become a teacher.

He had to thank former Gulls legend Don Mills for his breakthrough. Mills was scouting for United and spotted Twitchin playing in a five-a-side competition at Dawlish. He recommended him to the club and the Teignmouth Grammar School pupil was taken on as a schoolboy.

It was soon easy to see why he caught Mills' attention. With regular coaching, he progressed rapidly through United's youth set up and was good enough to win England Youth international honours.

In January 1970, he signed his first professional contract and by April had been given his first taste of League football in two fairly meaningless end-of-season games at Tranmere and Doncaster, with all the combatants stranded in mid-table with nothing to play for.

The following season saw Twitchin again involved in occasional first-team action, scoring his first league goal, against Bury, in only his fourth game. From mid-March, he played in every one of the remaining four-teen games, showing the versatility that would make him so invaluable in the future by playing in midfield or either full-back position.

Twitchin became the ideal club man. He would be the first to admit that he was not the most skilful of players but he was neat, compact and tenacious. Ask him to play in any position and he would with enthusiasm and give his all. He was not one for complaining but just got on with the job he was tasked with. There were no mazy dribbles, flying headers or histrionics, he just did what he had to do with the minimum of fuss.

Like any player, he was left out of the side on occasions. That hurt his personal pride and instilled a feeling that his performance must have let his team-mates down but, come Monday morning, he would train harder than anyone else and show his boss that he wanted his place back.

On the subject of training, Twitchin achieved legendary status within the confines of Plainmoor for his stamina on training runs. On the noto-rious 'Maidencombe run' Twitchin would invariably be out in front whilst others were, quite literally at times, falling by the wayside. Perversely, Twitchin seemed to enjoy this particular form of torture. Various meth-ods were used over the years to handicap him but it made little difference – he just kept on running.

One of his former managers, Mike Green, paid tribute to 'Twitch'. 'I've never seen anyone run like Twitch,' he says. 'No one could keep up with him in training and he was the same in a match. Quite often I used to tell him to take a breather. He would play anywhere as well. If I said 'I need you to play left wing this week,' he'd say "no problem boss". The next week I'd need him at right-back. Same response'.

As Green says, Twitchin has probably covered more miles than any other Torquay player. Had the Prozone system been invented in those times it would have undoubtedly shown Twitchin at the top of the 'yards run' column.

From December 1976 to May 1980, Twitchin embarked on a remark-able run of appearances, missing just three league games out of 167 in that period, winning the United 'Player of the Year' award in 1978.

At the end of the 1980-81 season, Twitchin was released. His final appearance had been his 400th in the League. The great shame was that, for all those miles he had run, all those tackles he had made, and all that sweat he had expelled, there were no trophies or medals to show for it. He had the misfortune to play during one of United's lengthy barren spells, but for him it was enough to have achieved his boyhood ambition and played professionally for his local club.

Like several ex-Gulls before him, Twitchin went on to play for Minehead. He still lives in his native Teignmouth.

Magic Moment: *Twitchin was rewarded for his loyalty when a star-studded Aston Villa side came to Plainmoor in August 1983 for his testimonial.*

Worst Nightmare: *In 1971, United were drawn at home to Spurs in the League Cup. United took a shock lead, but Spurs replied when Twitchin brought down Martin Chivers in the area when the ball appeared to be going harmlessly out of play. Martin Peters converted the resultant penalty and Spurs won 4-1.*

TORQUAY RECORD	Appearances	Goals
League	400	14
FA Cup	15	2
League Cup	20	1

No 27. **MIKE MAHONEY**

Debut: v Preston, 22 August 1970
Farewell: v Scunthorpe, 8 March 1975

Considering that Michael James Mahoney was brought to Plainmoor purely as goalkeeping cover, he became an ultra-reliable keeper who went on to have a successful career, and whose eventual departure possibly saved the club from going out of business.

Mahoney was born in Bristol on 25 October 1950 and joined Bristol City as an apprentice straight from school, eventually signing professional terms. He played just four games for the Ashton Gate club, having understudied the ever reliable Mike Gibson. 'Jock,' as he was also known, endured a torrid time with injuries. He developed a mysterious swelling on his knee, which led to exhaustive medical test and an operation. There was a fear he would never play again, but he fought his way back to fitness. Yet shortly after his comeback he suffered a broken jaw in a reserve game at Bournemouth.

Despite his injury record, Alan Brown brought him to Plainmoor, initially on loan, as cover for regular No 1, Andy Donnelly.

Donnelly was a consistent keeper who had been first choice for almost three seasons, but Mahoney was given an early opportunity when Donnelly was injured and he was drafted in for the second game of the 1970-71 season.

Mahoney's performances quickly belied his inexperience, to the extent that Donnelly was unable to regain his place and Brown was sufficiently impressed to make the move from Bristol permanent for a fee of £5,000.

Mahoney's run in the team soon came to an abrupt end. In a home game against Bristol Rovers at the end of November, he collided with an opponent and suffered a knee injury. Recovery was slow and in February it was decided that a cartilage operation was necessary. In modern times such a procedure is straightforward, causing minimal time out of the game, but in the early 1970s it was still considered major surgery with a lengthy rehabilitation time. Mahoney was out for the season.

He returned for the opening couple of games of the 1971-72 season, but the knee was still troublesome and disrupted another season in which he managed just thirteen appearances.

In the meantime, with the team struggling, Donnelly had suffered a crisis of confidence with John Connaughton brought in on loan from Manchester United.

By the start of the 1972-73 season, Donnelly had moved to South Africa. Mahoney had regained full fitness and was now unchallenged as United's first-choice keeper. The fans now saw him at his best. At 5ft 11ins, he was not big for a keeper, but he was brave and agile. The bushy haired, moustachioed figure would often fling himself full length to divert goal-bound shots. He played in every match, conceding just 47 goals, but the attack was equally goal-shy, leading to a disappointing eighteenth-place finish. Mahoney's efforts were rewarded with the club's 'Player of the Year' award.

The following season saw a similar pattern emerge. Mahoney missed just two games, was again voted 'Player of the Year', but the lack of an out-and-out goalscorer saw another mid-table finish. The club was also in increasing financial difficulties.

The financial plight came to a head in the 1974-75 season. United were knocked out of the FA Cup in the first round by Northampton, thus losing the opportunity for a money-spinning Cup run. This prompted chairman Tony Boyce to issue a public statement to the effect that unless the club received assistance from the council and supporters it could cease to exist.

The club had few disposable assets, but Mahoney was one of them, so when First Division Newcastle came along with an offer of £30,000 prior to the transfer deadline for the goalkeeper, it was not a difficult decision.

Mahoney was signed as cover for Iam McFaul, who was approaching retirement and quickly proved to be an adequate replacement for the Irish international. He played in the 1976 League Cup final at Wembley, when Manchester City's Dennis Tueart scored the winner with an overhead kick, and also played in the UEFA Cup.

Mahoney was a popular figure on Tyneside and formed a close friendship with Newcastle goalscoring legend Malcolm MacDonald. He also became friends with Newcastle speedway rider Mike Watkin. Mahoney helped in Watkin's testimonial events and was even let loose for a ride on Watkin's bike, not something a Premier League goalkeeper would be allowed to do in this day and age.

His best season at St James' Park was 1976-77, when Newcastle finished fifth in Division One. The following season, however, was a disastrous one. The Magpies collected just 22 points and were relegated with the worst defensive record in the division, conceding 78 goals. Mahoney's confidence was knocked badly and he eventually lost his first-team place, never to regain it, having notched up 135 appearances for the Magpies.

Mahoney was another of the exodus to soccer in the United States. In November 1978, he joined Chicago Sting for a £40,000 fee before moving on to California Surf. He settled in California, playing indoor soccer and helping to run soccer schools.

He remains there to this day and, until recently, has been playing in a veterans team called 'The Widebodies' – as a centre-half.

Magic Moment: *Mahoney's agility was exemplified with an unbelievable one-handed save against Leeds at Elland Road that denied striker, Duncan McKenzie a hat-trick.*

Worst Nightmare: *During a UEFA Cup-tie at Bohemians in Dublin in September 1977, the match was marred by ongoing crowd trouble. The start of the second half was delayed when Mahoney (and several policemen) were pelted with a variety of missiles.*

TORQUAY RECORD	Appearances	Goals
League	150	0
FA Cup	5	0
League Cup	5	0

No 28. **WILLIE BROWN**

Debut: v Rotherham, 18 March 1975
Farewell: v Southend, 18 April 1978

For the three full seasons that Willie Brown played for Torquay, he carried the mantle of top scorer. Indeed, his scoring record throughout his career is impressive, and it is a shame that he left the game when he had several good years in front of him.

William Brown was born in Falkirk on 5 February 1950. Despite his Scottish upbringing, he began his professional soccer life at Burnley, where he progressed through the junior ranks to turn pro in February 1967. However, he made just one substitute appearance for the first team, and the Clarets obviously believed he had little future in the game, letting him go on a free transfer to Carlisle in July 1969.

The Border club wanted Brown to gain some experience and, in September of that year, he played six games for Barrow, then a struggling Third Division side.

Brown scored his first League goal whilst on loan and returned to Carlisle a sharper and more streetwise player after his brief experience of League football. He fought his way into Carlisle's line up and ended the season with eight goals from nineteen appearances, but after a year at Brunton Park he moved again, this time to Newport. At least on this occasion Brown commanded a fee, albeit a modest £1,500.

Brown had hinted during his twelve months with Carlisle that he was capable of scoring on a regular basis and he further proved that at Newport. The club were perennial Fourth Division strugglers, but in Brown's first three years at Somerton Park they consistently improved their finishing position.

The South Wales fans really took to Brown, and he provided County's main source of goals. In 168 league games, he notched a half-century of goals, but towards the end of the 1973-74 season Brown found himself out of favour and in the March was sent on loan to Hereford. Again, Brown demonstrated his prowess, scoring six times in just nine games, but returned to Newport.

With seemingly little future at the Welsh club, a move was inevitable, and in November 1974 Brown moved to Brentford for £4,000. He failed to settle in the capital, although his record of nine goals in sixteen games for the Bees did little to suggest that.

With the March transfer deadline-day approaching, Torquay manager Malcolm Musgrove shelled out £5,000 of the club's hard-earned money to bring Brown to Plainmoor. Musgrove was desperate for someone who could put the ball in the net. United had been in freefall for some time, and it was easy to see why. In the eighteen matches prior to Brown's arrival, United had scored just nine times. The main source of goals had been midfielder Cliff Myers and Clint Boulton, who had spent much of the season at centre-half. A host of players had been tried up front, including the veteran Jim Fryatt, who is still credited with scoring the fastest goal in League football at four seconds. But Fryatt was clearly past his best, and played just three times in what was his second spell at Plainmoor.

The arrival of Brown, together with other new boys, Lew Chatterley, Steve Middleton and Pat Kruse, at least lifted spirits both on and off the pitch. United clocked up thirteen points and eighteen goals in their final eleven games and lifted themselves clear of danger.

The new campaign started brightly with a narrow home win over Workington, but United then proceeded to lose their next three league games, conceding thirteen goals in the process. Interspersed in this period was a thrilling 5-3 League Cup second-leg win over Swansea, with Brown and debutant Kevin Lane both scoring twice.

Gradually the team started to gel, although they still had their moments, losing 1-7 at Tranmere in October, but Musgrove was eventually able to field a reasonably settled side that would finish ninth, with seven players playing 40 games or more, including Brown, who played in every league game. He would also easily finish as top scorer with seventeen league and cup goals.

The 1976-77 league season started slowly for Brown. He did not score in a league game until 23 October, but he did take a liking to the League Cup, scoring all three goals that United managed in that competition, including a satisfying only goal of the game to knock his first side, Burnley – who included well-known names such as Keith Newton, Mike Summerbee and Brian Flynn – out of the competition.

Once Brown did get into his stride, there was no stopping him. In November, he scored five times in four games. The arrival of Colin Lee saw the duo strike up an immediately impressive partnership, with Lee's clever play and aerial ability the perfect foil for Brown's predator-like instincts. It would prove to be Brown's most productive season with a final tally of 22 league and cup goals.

Brown and Lee both scored in an opening-day win at Hartlepool in August 1977. United began the season with a potentially lethal three-pronged attack, with the lanky Les Lawrence joining the forward line as well. Again, Brown went through an early-season drought, but when Lee left for Spurs, he was again thrown the responsibility of the main goalscorer.

Brown again finished as top scorer with fourteen, but it was a shock when he quit the club at the end of the season. His manager of the time, Mike Green, had no inkling of his striker's impending departure. Earlier in the season, Brown had asked Green if he could assist with some coaching at the local technical college. The affable Green had no problems with the request. 'Willie always worked hard in training and I was happy for him to earn himself a few extra quid,' revealed Green. But there was a sting in the tail. At the end of the season, Brown told Green he was leaving to pursue his coaching.

Fellow striker Steve Cooper had recently joined the club, and one wonders what partnership the two would have formed, given time.

Brown then moved to Minehead, where he began a long association with that club, playing for them and then becoming their commercial manager. He settled in the Somerset seaside town and has run a newsagents there for many years.

Magic Moment: *Brown took little time in impressing his new employers, scoring on his debut for Torquay.*

Worst Nightmare: *Despite scoring, Brown was part of the first Torquay side to be knocked out of the FA Cup at home by a non-league side, when they were beaten 1-2 by Hillingdon Borough in November 1976.*

TORQUAY RECORD	Appearances	Goals
League	139	47
FA Cup	2	2
League Cup	13	7

No 29. **COLIN LEE**

Debut: v Huddersfield, 22 January 1977
Farewell: v Southport, 12 October 1978

Fans will always have their favourites, but a true testimony to a players ability is the appreciation of fellow professionals. Ask any number of former Torquay players of the mid-1970s to name the best player they played with, and the name of Colin Lee will regularly crop up.

Lee's playing career at Plainmoor was all too short, but in recent years he has played a significant role in off-the-field matters, and is now making a major contribution to restoring pride into the club after the most shambolic era in its history.

Lee was born in Plymouth on 12 June 1956 and played his early football at nearby Buckfastleigh, but his talents went unnoticed by the local League clubs and he joined Bristol City as an apprentice when he was sixteen, turning professional two years later. At school, Lee had another career in mind as a chef in the Merchant Navy, a somewhat strange choice for someone who confesses to suffer from seasickness. He was also a promising rugby player and was picked for Devon on the same day he was due for a trial at Bristol City.

As a centre-forward, Lee was unable to break into City's first team, but he did make his league debut during this period when he was loaned to Hereford during the 1974-75 season, playing nine games without scoring.

At Plainmoor, the United fans had endured yet another poor start to the season, culminating in a disastrous 1-2 defeat at home to Hillingdon Borough, the Gulls' first ever home defeat to non-league opposition in the Cup. This, and rumours of ill-discipline among some players, had cost affable manager Malcolm Musgrove his job, and chairman Tony Boyce had persuaded Frank O'Farrell to return to the hot seat.

O'Farrell immediately set out to strengthen the side. It was not difficult to see where his priority lay. Willie Brown aside, United couldn't score goals. Although inexperienced, Lee was available and cheap, and would add much-needed aerial power to the United forward line.

After just one win in seven games, Lee was soon handed a starting place, scoring on his debut. He scored in his next match, too. He began to find the back of the net regularly, forming a good partnership with Brown, who finished as top scorer with 22 league and cup goals. Lee also managed double figures in just 23 games. The next highest goalscorer was midfield player Lew Chatterley with four, and that included a late season hat-trick.

For the start of the next season, the tall figure of Les Lawrence had joined Lee and Brown in the forward line to give it a more robust look, but the trio failed to hit it off immediately and again the Gulls got off to a disappointing start.

Despite this, Lee had caught the eye of other clubs. There was much more to his game than his heading prowess. His movement, close control and intelligent link up play were all impressive. It was still a shock, however, that a major side like Tottenham should come in for a player with only 40-odd League games under his belt.

Under manager Keith Burkinshaw, Spurs had been relegated to the old Second Division. Not only that, they were suffering an injury crisis, and so Lee's arrival at White Hart Lane for £60,000 was timely. Two days after signing, he made a sensational debut, scoring four times in a 9-0 annihilation of Bristol Rovers, a match also televised on *Match of the Day*.

Obviously it was impossible for Lee to maintain such standards and his headline-making debut soon alerted opposing sides, but he held his place in a side that scraped back to the First Division on goal-difference at their first attempt.

The fact that Lee also held onto his first-team slot on a regular basis in the First Division underlined his quality. He played a total of 71 games for Spurs, scoring 21 times, and was also used at times in defence.

In January 1980 a £20,000 fee took him to Chelsea, managed at the time by Geoff Hurst. A persistent hamstring injury dogged his early days at Stamford Bridge but he eventually established himself in the Blues forward line and found success being part of the side who won promotion from the Second Division in 1984 and the Full Members' Cup two years later, when he scored twice in the final. He was never a prolific scorer but netted some important goals and notched a hat-trick in a 6-0 win over Newcastle.

Injuries and illness continued to hamper his progress at Chelsea and a spell on the sidelines allowed David Speedie the opportunity to partner the prolific Kerry Dixon in attack. Lee reinvented himself as a full-back, replacing the ageing John Hollins, but his hamstrings continued to trouble him and after seven years with the Blues he was sold to Brentford in July 1987 for £17,500, where he also took on the role of youth development officer.

Lee always had an interest in coaching and his playing days came to an end in 1989. He took up the post of youth-team coach at Watford and replaced Steve Harrison as manager in March 1990, but the perils of football management first hit him when he was sacked in the following November after a poor start to the new campaign.

He then returned to a youth-coach role at Reading, later becoming assistant manager with the Royals under Mark McGhee. He followed McGhee to both Leicester and Wolves, and when McGhee was sacked by the Molineux club he was promoted to manage the side. His first game in charge saw a particularly satisfying 6-1 win over Bristol City. For two seasons, Wolves narrowly missed out on the Division One play-offs and in December 2000 Lee was fired.

He was employed as a scout for Leeds when, in March 2001, he received a call from Torquay chairman Mike Bateson. United were facing relegation to the Conference and Bateson offered Lee the chance to act as a consultant to under-pressure manager Wes Saunders. Lee accepted and within a couple of weeks found himself managing the side after Saunders had been sacked.

Lee achieved the task he had been given, as United avoided the drop on the last day. During the close season he was offered the role permanently but, in early July with a contract in front of him, he declined the job, leaving United managerless a week before pre-season training was due to resume.

Lee returned to his scouting work for Leeds, as well as doing some radio and TV work. In December 2001 he was appointed as a coach at Wigan, before another managerial role, this time at Walsall, came his way within a couple of months.

He remained with the Midlands club until March 2004, when he was sacked in bizarre circumstances. He had been given permission to speak to Plymouth about the managerial vacancy at Home Park. Lee publicly turned the job down but was then sacked by the Walsall chairman who claimed that if Lee was totally committed to his job he wouldn't have even spoken to Argyle and dismissed him for misconduct! Eventually, the League Managers; Association intervened and Lee's contract was paid up.

Unperturbed by such events, he took on another challenge when he became Millwall boss in July 2005, replacing Steve Claridge who had been sacked after just 36 days. In December of that year, he was 'moved upstairs' to become director of football, but left a few weeks later.

In January 2007 he made another return to Plainmoor as coach. This was now a club in crisis for many reasons, and with an inexperienced manager in Lubos Kubik. Kubik didn't last long. Lee was given temporary charge of the side before being given the official role of director of football, where his first move was to bring in Keith Curle as manager.

Of course, United couldn't be saved from relegation to the Conference and in May 2007, when Bateson stood down as chairman, Lee was made redundant. He wasn't gone for long. Within days, the club had been sold to a local consortium which saw sense and made Lee the new chief executive, a role he remains in and fulfils with great passion and enthusiasm, and which has been rewarded with United restoring their League status and becoming a respected club again.

Magic Moment: *Lee masterminded a nervy, final-day 3-2 win at Barnet in May 2001 to save United from relegation and send Barnet down. Thousands were locked out of the tiny Underhill ground.*

Worst Nightmare: *Lee was stunned when he was informed that he would not be required to continue as director of football at Torquay in May 2007, describing the situation as 'disgusting'.*

TORQUAY RECORD	Appearances	Goals
League	35	14
FA Cup	0	0
League Cup	3	1

No 30. **LES LAWRENCE**

Debut: v Hartlepool, 20 August 1977
Farewell: v Darlington, 18 May 1982

Les Lawrence had a nomadic existence as a player, but it was at Torquay where he enjoyed his longest and most successful spell at one club.

Leslie Oliver Lawrence was born in Rowley Regis on 18 May 1957. As a youngster at Springfield Secondary Modern School, he was a good all round sportsman and looked to have a promising cricket career ahead of him as a fast bowler. He was good enough to represent Staffordshire schools but football was always his number one game.

Even at school, Lawrence towered above his schoolmates. His height made him an obvious choice as a centre-half but it was as a striker, scoring goals, that he was most comfortable. He joined Aston Villa as a schoolboy from the age of twelve, but was eventually released and began his senior football career at Stourbridge.

In 1975, he was signed by Shrewsbury, but spent a frustrating two years there with his first-team opportunities limited. At the end of the 1976-77 season he was released and actually signed for Telford, but never played for them.

At Plainmoor, manager Mike Green was busy constructing a new-look side that he hoped would challenge for honours. Lawrence was one of a number of new signings and made his debut in the opening game of the 1977-78 season.

Lawrence was initially part of a three-pronged attack, alongside Willie Brown and Colin Lee, although Lee was soon on his way. It was also to be Brown's last season, although he and Lawrence began to form a useful partnership. Lawrence racked up 34 appearances during that season, gaining useful experience.

The following season saw Lawrence miss just one game and finish as United's top scorer with nineteen league and cup goals. His partnership with new strike duo Steve Cooper and Donal Murphy began to flourish, with the trio notching up 44 goals between them.

Lawrence's strength was his aerial ability. At 6ft 3ins, he was a handful for any defender and possessed a remarkable leap, once measured at four feet from a standing jump.

It is the image of Lawrence that is perhaps most enduring. He was United's first coloured player and, with a thick 'afro' hairstyle and Mexican moustache, he was instantly recognisable. Indeed, in each season's team picture, the hair seems to get bigger and bigger.

The following season saw the triumvirate score 46 times, with Lawrence contributing seventeen. His partnership with Cooper, in particular, was beginning to attract the attention of other clubs, with Ipswich boss Bobby Robson taking a particular interest. Lawrence's all-round game had improved, thanks to additional coaching from veteran striker John Rudge, who was Green's assistant.

Despite possessing such a lethal strike-force, United could not make a push for promotion. The 1980-81 season started disappointingly for both Lawrence and United. Inconsistency blighted the campaign and after a 0-2 defeat at Bradford in early February the unthinkable happened, when both Lawrence and Cooper were dropped.

The lack of progress cost Green his job at the end of the season. Frank O'Farrell returned for his third spell as manager, with Bruce Rioch employed as player-coach with a view to succeeding his manager in due course.

With Lawrence and Cooper restored to the attack, the new season started promisingly but, again, United flattered to deceive and started to slide down the table. Among the moves made to stem the losing run was to play Lawrence at centre-back. His height and aerial power were useful but he was not particularly happy there. Nevertheless, it was a shock to him and the supporters when he was released at the end of the season.

Thus commenced a journey around various clubs. Port Vale, Aldershot, Rochdale and Burnley were all on the Lawrence radar before a £10,000 fee took him to Peterborough where he made a scoring debut. But a ruptured Achilles which necessitated three operations disrupted any thoughts of a regular berth.

Cambridge became his final League club. Injuries took their toll and, although he was offered the opportunity to coach there, Lawrence decided to make a clean break from League football. He played non-league for a variety of clubs – Kettering, Aylesbury, Corby and Bourne before a spell as manager of Spalding.

After football, Lawrence went into sales, spending twelve months with a cane furniture importer. He was then appointed as an area sales manager for Pirelli Tyres, progressing to a director, necessitating regular business trips to Italy. He remained with the company for sixteen years and in 2004 moved to rival firm Bridgestone, where he is now head of commercial sales in the UK.

As well as his hectic business life, Lawrence has also found time to be captain of his golf club near his home in Market Deeping. He rarely gets the time to watch live football these days, but still takes a keen interest in Torquay's results. After all, he reflects that his time at Plainmoor was the happiest of his football career. He enjoyed the Friday night home games, the most productive spell of his career, and he met his wife whilst a United player. And no, he no longer has that afro hairstyle.

Magic Moment: *Lawrence scored a hat-trick at Plainmoor in a 3-2 win over Barnsley on 31 January 1979. He still has the match ball.*

Worst Nightmare: *After the above match, Barnsley manager Allan Clarke (the ex-Leeds and England striker) was so upset with the result that he refused to sign the match ball. His assistant, Norman Hunter, signed it on his behalf.*

TORQUAY RECORD	Appearances	Goals
League	189	46
FA Cup	10	4
League Cup	13	4

Wing wizard Ron Shaw lets fly during
Torquay's 2-0 home win over Walsall in
September 1954. Harold Dobbie is behind

Torquay record appearance holder
Kevin Hill played 458 games for United

Goalscoring hero Robin Stubbs leaving
Plainmoor for the last time as a Torquay player

Sammy Collins almost takes the Reading keeper's head off
during this 2-0 home win in April 1953

Tommy Northcott climbs above Alan Mullery during the 3-3 draw in the FA Cup-tie
against Spurs in January 1965. Watching in the background for Torquay is Geoff Cox

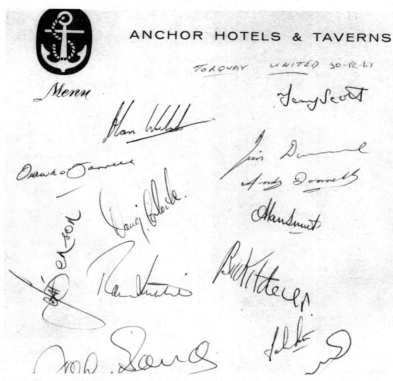

ANCHOR HOTELS & TAVERNS

Torquay players and officials attended the Anchor Hotel on 30 December 1967.
How many signatures can you recognise?

Boxing Day at Oxford. Robin Stubbs seeks refuge behind the referee
as Ron Atkinson is restrained by brother Graham

Ken Sandercock followed Frank O'Farrell to Leicester City in November 1969

Les Lawrence was Torquay's leading scorer in season 1978-79

Robin Stubbs (right) with trainer Happy Topping

Tony Scott was signed from West Ham

Full-back Bob Glozier

Torquay beat Plymouth 3-2 at Plainmoor in December 1951, their first ever League win over their Devon rivals

Sammy Collins in the thick of it at home to Aldershot in this 4-0 win in January 1950

CHURCHMAN'S CIGARETTES

Don Welsh, then in his Charlton days, in this series of cigarette cards

ASSOCIATION FOOTBALLERS

A SERIES OF 50

46

D. WELSH
(Charlton Athletic)

Chosen five times as a reserve for England, Donald Welsh played in the matches against Germany and Switzerland at the end of the 1937/38 season, and he ranks as one of the leading left-halves. Born in Manchester, he joined the Navy at the age of sixteen and on leaving the Service played for Torquay United as an amateur. In the following season he turned professional and, in February, 1935, was transferred to Charlton at a fee of £3,250, the highest ever paid by this club. He helped to win promotion to the Second, and then to the First Division, playing both as a centre- and wing-half and also as a centre-forward. He is a bold attacking player with a strong shot.

Torquay United v Plymouth Argyle
Tony Bedeau's Testimonial
Saturday, July 16, 2005

Torquay United

Head coach:
Leroy Rosenior

Andy Marriott
Matt Hockley
Matt Hewlett
Craig Taylor
Tony Bedeau
Darren Garner
Leon Constantine
Jo Kuffour
Kevin Hill
James Bittner
Martin Phillips
Matt Villis
Nick Skinner
Brian McGlinchey
Steve Woods
Liam Coleman
Alan Connell
Alex Lawless

Special guest:
Neville Southall

Plymouth Argyle

Manager:
Bobby Williamson

■ Romain Larrieu
■ Lee Hodges
■ Taribo West
■ Keith Lasley
■ David Norris
■ Akos Buzskay
■ Micky Evans
■ Bjarni Gudjonsson
■ Mathias Doumbe
■ Tony Capaldi
■ Paul Wotton
■ Hasney Aljofree
■ Nick Chadwick
■ Scott Taylor
■ Paul Connolly
■ Luke McCormick
■ Peter Gilbert
■ Ryan Dickson
■ Luke Summerfield
■ Anthony Barness
■ Rufus Brevett
■ Bojan Djordjic

Referee: Trevor Parkes
Assistant referees: Mike Mullarkey & Andy Turner
Fourth official: Jason Heywood

Remaining Torquay United pre-season friendlies at Plainmoor:
Charlton Athletic - Tuesday, July 19, 7.45pm
Nottingham Forest - Saturday, July 30, 3pm

No 31. **STEVE COOPER**

Debut: v Huddersfield, 8 March 1978
Farewell: v Blackpool, 12 May 1984

Fans like nothing more than a player who can score goals, a player who gives 100 per cent, and a player who battles tooth and nail from the first whistle to the last. With Steven Milne Cooper, Torquay supporters had all three rolled into one. It is not surprising therefore that he became one of the most popular players of recent times.

Cooper was born on 14 December 1955 and brought up on a council estate in Stourbridge. Despite a relatively poor upbringing, he had bags of ability as a goalscoring striker. He caught the eye playing for Stourbridge and was given an opportunity by Brighton. He was in fact Brian Clough's first signing at the Goldstone Ground.

At first, things looked promising when Cooper was involved in first-team pre-season friendlies. He still recalls being scared to death of the Clough-Peter Taylor partnership, which ruled with an iron fist, to the extent of sending a trainee home when he was caught yawning during training.

But events soon took a turn for the worse at Brighton. Clough and Taylor had an infamous and well publicised falling out. Clough left for his 44-day reign at Leeds, leaving Taylor in charge. Determined to make his mark after spending years as Clough's number two, Taylor virtually ostracised all the players Clough had brought in. Cooper was sent to Southern League Dover for a loan spell but soon returned to Stourbridge.

A number of clubs showed an interest in Cooper but, on the advice of his father, he eventually signed for Torquay in early 1978. United player-manager Mike Green was beginning to build an entertaining side but lacked an out and out goalscorer to turn them into genuine promotion candidates.

Cooper was eventually given his first-team opportunity and had a stormer on his debut. He retained his place for the next two games but on heavy pitches he struggled and was left out again.

He returned at the end of March and, on firmer surfaces, he looked a different player. He scored three times in the final six games and began to forge a promising strike partnership with Les Lawrence. United won their final three games of the season, which gave hope for the following season.

The 1978-79 season did indeed start promisingly, with Cooper, Lawrence and new signing, Donal Murphy all finding the net regularly, but inconsistency set in and a mid-table finish was disappointing, given the pre-season anticipation. The aforementioned triumvirate scored a combined 45 league and cup goals, but received little support, the remainder of the side managing just nineteen between them. Cooper's individual tally of fifteen goals would probably have been more, but he regularly missed games through niggling injuries, perhaps not surprising given his combative and fearless approach to each game.

For the 1979-80 season, Green concentrated on strengthening his defence, the area of the side that had let him down previously. United were considered one of the favourites for promotion and their early form justified such claims. The attractive style of play was still there and the side scored freely, with the three main protagonists from the previous campaign again regularly on the scoresheet. Cooper netted a hat-trick against Darlington and, by the New Year, United were well in the promotion hunt.

After an away win at Bournemouth it suddenly started to go wrong. United went fifteen games without winning, scuppering any thoughts of promotion. For Cooper, it was a successful season. He finished as leading scorer with twenty goals and started to attract attention from other clubs. Chelsea were rumoured to be interested but Cooper was enjoying life at Torquay and, to his credit, was never particularly interested in moving on. He had few rivals in winning United's 'Player of the Year' award.

Many of Cooper's goals came from headers. He was not particularly tall but could leap like a salmon.

Another mediocre season cost Green his job and Bruce Rioch came in as player-manager. Cooper continued to give his usual commitment to the cause but admits he did not always see eye to eye with the ways of his new boss.

No game epitomised the effort that Cooper expended better than a fourth round FA Cup-tie at First Division Sheffield Wednesday in January 1983. Owls boss Jack Charlton, a man who knew a thing or two about centre-forwards, had done his homework and earmarked Cooper for special attention. Wednesday scraped through with a narrow 3-2 win, but World Cup winner Charlton admitted afterwards that his defenders could not cope with the Torquay No 9, who could 'put himself about a bit'.

When Rioch resigned midway through the 1983-84 season, David Webb took over. Gradually the old brigade were wheeled out, with several untried youngsters brought in. It was to prove to be Cooper's last season. He had already been sent to see a Harley Street specialist about ankle problems and faced the stark warning that if he carried on playing he could end up in a wheelchair.

For all his unstinting loyalty to the club, Cooper had a raw deal. He ended up receiving minimal compensation for his injury. There was no mention of any testimonial, and there are no medals to look back on. What he did was to give pleasure to thousands of fans over his Torquay career.

After his professional playing days were over, Cooper played part time for a while at Saltash. For several years now he has been running his pub, the Maltster's Arms at Clyst St Mary near Exeter.

Magic Moment: *On 25 April 1979, Cooper scored the first of two hat-tricks in his League career in a 3-0 home win over York. Sadly, only just over 1,500 people were at Plainmoor to witness it.*

Worst Nightmare: *In a 'friendly' against Plymouth Argyle, Cooper was forced to go off and have nine stitches administered to a head wound.*

TORQUAY RECORD	Appearances	Goals
League	234	76
FA Cup	17	7
League Cup	15	4

No 32. **JOHN TURNER**

Debut: v Northampton, 19 August 1978
Farewell: v Chesterfield, 18 March 1984

Of the several fine goalkeepers United have had guarding their goal over the years, John Graham Anthony Turner would rank among the best. Perhaps the most apt tribute comes from fans of Peterborough, his last League club, many of whom believed him to be as good as, if not better than, the man he replaced, a certain David Seaman.

Turner was born in Peterlee on 23 December 1954 and lived in the nearby village of Horden. The local community was dominated by the mining industry, and the young Turner seemed destined to do what most of the male population did in that area – work in the mines, but Turner was a talented young goalkeeper

Turner was playing for Easington, coincidentally the birthplace of Jimmy Trotter, a prolific Torquay United forward of the 1930s, when he was offered an opportunity at Derby County. He successfully graduated from the apprentice ranks to sign a professional contract at the Baseball Ground in December 1972.

It was the era of Brian Clough, and Turner has many an amusing story to tell of Clough's legendary antics. The young player and the charismatic manager got on well. Clough called Turner 'Young John'. Clough enjoyed working with and developing the young pros and Turner recalls making his manager numerous cups of tea, mowing his lawn and even helping him move house.

Back on the field, Turner was impressing everyone. He became a regular in the Derby reserve side, winning two Central League titles and was voted the best goalkeeper in the annual Toulon Under-23 tournament in France.

A first-team opportunity at Derby passed him by, however, and he went on loan to Doncaster in February 1974 (saving a penalty on his League debut).

Another loan spell at Brighton followed. A certain Brian Clough was by this time managing the Seagulls, and Turner felt confident that his old boss would give him a chance but, of course, Clough left to take up his infamous 44-day stint as manager of Leeds, and Turner returned to Derby.

Further loan spells followed at Peterborough and Huddersfield but, in May 1975, Reading paid £2,000 to take Turner to Elm Park as cover for Steve Death. Turner quickly became popular with the fans and not just for his on-the-field exploits as part of Reading's promotion winning side. He was always willing to promote the interests of the club around the area, coached a number of local sides, and even became part of the Supporters Club quiz team.

Despite this, Turner never managed to really usurp the legendary Death as first choice No 1, and in the summer of 1978, he signed for Torquay for £3,000 replacing the Newport-bound Terry Lee.

Turner quickly impressed. He was a fitness fanatic, and his agility saw him regularly pull off some stunning saves. He played in every match and claimed the club's 'Player of the Year' accolade.

The next season saw United become outside candidates for promotion. They recovered from some early-season hiccups to hit a good run of form. Turner was again an automatic choice, with his reputation growing. In February 1980, the ambitious Chesterfield offered £50,000 for him. It was too good an offer to refuse.

He soon encountered success, gaining an Anglo-Scottish Cup winners medal. The run to the final included an unlikely two-leg victory over Glasgow Rangers, with Turner saving a penalty in the home tie. This was the last season in which the competition was held, and so the Spireites still hold the trophy in their cabinet.

Turner was now rated as one of the best keepers in the lower divisions, and had a brief loan spell at Everton, so it was something of a coup when United managed to re-sign him for the start of the 1983-84 season. He again produced a string of impressive performances but when David Webb replaced Bruce Rioch as manager he quickly started bringing in players from his former club, Bournemouth. Among them was goalkeeper Kenny Allen, who was immediately handed the keeper's jersey. Allen was an able deputy, but the move did little to endear Webb to the supporters.

Turner joined Weymouth, but found himself at Burnley for the start of the new season. Within two months he had been transferred to Peterborough to replace Seaman. He played 70 times for the Posh but his League career was ended in January 1986 when, on a snowy London Road pitch, he suffered a broken leg in an FA Cup-tie against Leeds.

Following his retirement from League football, Turner returned to live in Torquay, taking over the 'Fortune of War' pub near Plainmoor. He played for several years for local side Waldon Athletic. In April 1991, he returned to the club as youth coach and assistant to new manager John Impey, but the pair were sacked the following October after a string of poor results.

In 2006, he was asked to help coach United's keepers on a part-time basis, under the ill-fated and short reign of the Czech, Lubos Kubik.

After running several different pubs around the area, Turner has now settled at the Jolly Sailor in the village of Ogwell near Newton Abbot. He is a keen golfer, is probably the slimmest publican you will find, and still regularly attends matches at Plainmoor.

Turner's brother, Robbie was a striker who played for no less than twelve different League clubs.

Magic Moment: *During a match for Derby reserves, Turner injured his hand and could not continue in goal. He moved outfield and promptly scored a hat-trick.*

Worst Nightmare: *Playing against Wimbledon! In his first season at Torquay, Turner conceded six at home and five away against the Londoners.*

TORQUAY RECORD	Appearances	Goals
League	110	0
FA Cup	7	0
League Cup	10	0

No 33. **COLIN ANDERSON**

Debut: v Darlington, 18 September 1982
Farewell: v Mansfield, 19 March 1985

Like John Turner, Colin Russell Anderson is a product of the North East. Born in Newcastle on 26 April 1962, Anderson's move to Plainmoor resurrected a career that seemed to be sliding into oblivion.

Anderson's football career began at Burnley. He joined the Turf Moor club as an apprentice, turning professional in April 1980. Six months later, he made his first-team debut against Fulham at Craven Cottage, but he was largely on the periphery and, after just six first-team appearances in total, he was released. He returned briefly to the North East, playing for North Shields, but in September 1982 was brought to Plainmoor by manager Bruce Rioch for a two-week trial.

United's finances were in their usual parlous state and Rioch's squad threadbare as a consequence, and so players of Anderson's ilk – available for nothing and cheap to employ – fitted the bill as far as any potential new intake was concerned. To Anderson's amazement, within days of his arrival he was thrust into first-team action. What was more surprising was that Rioch's ragbag bunch had actually started the season in encouraging fashion. Anderson's debut resulted in a 1-0 win which put United top of the table, unbeaten in five games.

Given his relative inexperience, Anderson took to League football like a duck to water. Used as a midfield player, Anderson, a left footer, showed great energy in his play, covering up and down the pitch. The decision to offer him a permanent contract was an easy one and he went on to play in every remaining game of that first season.

Unfortunately, United couldn't maintain that early-season momentum, finishing mid-table, but Anderson's committed all-action displays saw the fans take him to their hearts, and at the end of the campaign he was voted as 'Player of the Year'.

The start to the following season was in complete contrast. Despite a number of new signings, the Gulls were bottom after six games. Anderson was again a model of consistency. The signing of Keith Curle from Bristol Rovers seemed to be a turning point. Curle would be a future England international defender, but it was as a winger that he initially made his mark with Torquay, scoring three goals in his first three games as Rioch's side gradually climbed the table.

The revival came to an abrupt halt with mid-season defeats at Crewe and Tranmere. These losses preceded an incident that Anderson was

directly involved in, and one which apparently shocked those who witnessed it.

A frustrated Rioch had been particularly unhappy with the performance of certain players in the Tranmere defeat, Anderson included. Rioch
understandably aired his views in the dressing room. but by the time the
players reported back for training on the Monday, the manager had not
cooled off. At a team meeting, Anderson was again the focus of his ire.
The squad went to Audley Park for a training session and, during a five-
a-side game, Rioch subjected Anderson to a heavy tackle in which
Anderson banged his head on a wall, virtually knocking himself out.
According to eye witnesses, Rioch then set about Anderson whilst he lay
prone on the ground. Other players pulled him off, but Rioch launched
a second attack.

A dazed and confused Anderson was taken to hospital but later
allowed home. Within hours, the PFA were on the case, demanding
action and scuppering any thoughts that the club could keep the matter
'in house' and hope to patch things up.

With the PFA involvement, Rioch was forced to resign but the shock-
ing and unsavoury incident cast a shadow over the club.

Rioch's replacement was Dave Webb, who quickly brought in a number of new personnel. Indeed, the line up for the final game of the season contained just two players – Anderson and John Impey – who had
started the first game. To his credit, Anderson had been unaffected by the
events surrounding him. He missed just seven games and, under Webb,
again demonstrated his versatility, playing at left-back for the second half
of the season.

Despite another poor start to the 1984-85 season, Anderson's stock
was still rising. He was one of the few successes in a team that was
chopped and changed week in, week out, with little success. The Torquay
public had also taken an indifferent attitude to the plight of its football
team, and crowds hovered around the one-thousand mark for a number
of games. It was clear to all that Anderson would move on to better
things. He had a number of suitors but in the end signed for First
Division West Brom, initially on loan in March 1985. The move was soon
made permanent, but the fee of £25,000 was derisory, leaving many fans
fuming that he had not commanded a figure commensurate with his considerable ability.

Anderson made his First Division debut early in the 1985-86 season,
when he came on as a substitute against Everton at Goodison Park. He
soon established himself in the Baggies' first-choice line up. He was a
solid performer, never spectacular, but the type of player his fellow pros

and managers admired. He remained at the Hawthorns until the summer of 1991, notching twelve goals in 152 appearances.

A series of free transfers followed, to Walsall, Hereford, and Exeter. Despite his Geordie roots, Anderson enjoyed the Devon lifestyle and settled back in the area. He played local non-league football for Dawlish and Teignmouth, and still lives in the area, where he runs his own carpentry and joinery business.

Magic Moment: *Anderson won back-to-back Torquay Player of the Year awards in 1983 and 1984.*

Worst Nightmare: *When Bruce Rioch was given the high-profile Arsenal manager's job, the tabloid press resurrected the training ground incident story and hounded Anderson to give his version of events. He resisted any approaches.*

TORQUAY RECORD	Appearances	Goals
League	109	10
FA Cup	7	1
League Cup	5	0

No 34. **DEREK DAWKINS**

Debut: v Wrexham, 18 February 1984
Farewell: v Scunthorpe, 26 November 1988

There have been few more popular players to have donned a Torquay shirt than Derek Anthony Dawkins, more affectionately known as 'The Dude'.

Born in Edmonton, London on 29 November 1959, Dawkins had a fairly unremarkable career up to the point of joining the Gulls. He had started life as an apprentice at Leicester and was good enough to be given a professional contract in November 1977. He was given his first-team opportunity in the final three games of that season, with City already relegated, but he allowed to move on and signed for Mansfield in December 1978.

He became more of a regular at Mansfield's Field Mill, clocking up 73 appearances before being released at the conclusion of the 1980-81 season. He joined Bournemouth, managed at the time by David Webb, but Webb was sacked a few months later, and Dawkins drifted into non-league football with Weymouth after only eight appearances for the Cherries.

Dawkins' career was thrown a lifeline in February 1984 when Webb was appointed manager at Plainmoor following the resignation of Bruce Rioch. The new man quickly set about making his mark, signing Dawkins and Paul Compton, another of his ex-Bournemouth charges. Over the following weeks a stream of new faces arrived at the club, with some of the high-earning but popular players allowed to leave, a move which did not endear the new boss to the supporters. Several of his new signings were ex-Bournemouth players who had won promotion in 1982. Webb believed they could gel and do the same for United.

Dawkins did not allow the politics of the situation affect him. He was grateful for another opportunity in League football and quickly settled into his midfield role.

The following season was a disastrous one for the club. Players came and went with increasing regularity. Webb brought in ageing stars, such as Tony Currie and Eddie Kelly. He even picked himself at the age of almost 39. Amid the turmoil, Dawkins was one of the few players to emerge with any credit, being the only ever present in a side that finished bottom of the Football League and forced to seek re-election. Dawkins' versatility came to the fore in a mid-season injury crisis which saw him play in a variety of positions.

Another bottom place finished followed and, in 1986-87, with League rules changed to ensure the bottom side were relegated, United looked favourites to go down until the famous last-day escape thanks, in part, to Bryn the police dog. Dawkins played a large part in the final day draw against Crewe to ensure survival when he was asked to play at centre-half, a relatively unfamiliar position for him, but one in which he performed admirably.

Earlier in the season, Dawkins had experienced his greatest moment in a United shirt. He did not score many goals, preferring to do the dirty work in the side in his usual unspectacular and efficient manner, but United were handed a plum two-legged tie against Spurs in the League Cup. A capacity 4,999 crammed into Plainmoor to see stars such as Ray Clemence, Gary Mabbutt and Chris Waddle perform and hope to witness a shock result.

The home leg seemed to be heading for a goalless draw, a more than respectable result for United, but with three minutes remaining, Plainmoor erupted. Dawkins ghosted into the penalty area and fired past a hapless Clemence to seal an historic win. 'The Dude' was chaired off the pitch shoulder high by a sea of ecstatic fans. His balding head had never shone so bright under the Plainmoor lights. His smile had never been wider.

There was no fairy tale end. United lost the second leg 0-2 at White Hart Lane, but Dawkins goal etched him into Torquay folklore. He was already a massively popular figure with the fans and now he was afforded cult status. His 'Dude' nickname came about because of 'cool' style of dress.

By this time, he had also been given extra responsibilities. With teammate Sean Haselgrave, he was asked to train the club's youngsters and one of his early charges was a young Lee Sharpe, who in his autobiography describes the tortuous routine he was put through.

Having reached his 30s and with niggling injuries, Dawkins' playing days at Plainmoor inevitably came to an end. He moved to Newport County, just prior to the winding up of the club due to financial difficulties, and did not manage to play a game for the Welsh side. He subsequently played for Yeovil and Gloucester City. There was hope that the Dawkins legacy would live on at Plainmoor when his son, Luke, was taken on as an apprentice, but he was eventually released.

Dawkins returned to live in Torquay, where he ran a business selling mobile phone accessories. In recent years he has put his experience and enthusiasm for football to good use as a coach for the Sheffield United Soccer Academy in Southern Spain, but he will long be remembered at Torquay.

Magic Moment: *Dawkins' enduring popularity at Plainmoor is such that 'The Dude' t-shirts are still available to purchase!*

Worst Nightmare: *Due to a shortage of players, Dawkins was forced to play in a match at Burnley in April 1987 with a broken wrist.*

Torquay record	Appearances	Goals
League	175	7
FA Cup	12	0
League Cup	8	2

No 35. **KENNY ALLEN**

Debut: v Hartlepool, 17 March 1984
Farewell: v Bolton, 28 May 1989

Standing at 6ft 4ins, and with a shock of grey hair and the trademark moustache, Kenneth Richard Allen was an instantly recognisable figure between the posts for Torquay in the 1980s.

Born in the north-eastern town of Thornaby on Tees on 12 January 1952, Allen began his senior football carer at Tow Law Town, a club that was to later produce Chris Waddle.

In August 1986, he joined Hartlepool as an amateur, playing seven League games before he embarked on a four-year spell in South Africa, playing for the Hellenic club.

After returning to these shores, he had brief spells with both West Brom and Workington without making a first-team appearance and, when a move to Bath City came about in September 1973, it appeared to signal the end of any hopes of returning to the Football League.

Allen remained for five years at Twerton Park, where he became something of a legend and was reckoned to be one of the best keepers ever to play for the club. He enjoyed success there, with the club winning promotion in 1973-74, and the Southern League title four years later. In total he played 280 games for Bath.

In August 1978, Allen broke back into League football when he moved to Bournemouth for £7,000 as a replacement for Kieron Baker. Further honours came his way at Dean Court with a successful 1981-82 promotion campaign.

Being a keeper is, of course, a hazardous occupation, as Allen has found out on more than one occasion.

A week prior to Christmas 1982 he was between the sticks for Bournemouth's record and farcical defeat – 0-9 at Lincoln.

It was Harry Redknapp's first game in charge as caretaker manager of the south-coast club. The side had departed from Bournemouth on a chilly but sunny and bright Friday for the trip to Lincolnshire, but by the Saturday conditions had changed. On arriving at Sincil Bank, the Cherries found a frozen pitch. Despite Redknapp's best efforts the referee decreed that the game would go ahead. The Bournemouth players only had their normal studded boots at their disposal and in the warm up realised they were in trouble.

The Lincoln players wore pimpled trainers and ran rings around their opponents. The goalmouths were particularly affected, and after twenty minutes, Allen improvised by discarding his boots, donning a second pair of socks and played the rest of the match attired as such.

For 90 minutes, wave after wave of Lincoln attacks bore down on Allen's goal. He pulled off numerous saves and by the end was happy to keep the score down to nine.

In September 1979, he was on the end of another bizarre incident, at Tranmere. With Bournemouth beating the home side 4-0, an elderly, extremely disgruntled Rovers fan whacked Allen across the backside with a walking stick.

On another occasion, Allen was attacked by a fan when playing for Torquay at Peterborough.

Allen remained a Bournemouth player until 1983, notching up 152 League appearances before he was off on his travels again. After brief unsuccessful spells at Bury and Peterborough, without playing a first-team game, he tried his luck in Sweden with IFK Gothenburg.

March 1984 heralded Allen's arrival at Plainmoor, signed by Gulls boss David Webb, who had managed Allen at Bournemouth and seemed intent on packing his new Torquay side with ex-Cherries. Allen was immediately drafted into the side, replacing the popular John Turner, and made his United debut at his first League club, Hartlepool, although only 969 fans turned up to witness the event.

The following season saw Allen miss just three games, but he was kept busy as United finished finished bottom of the Football League, forcing the club to seek re-election for the first time since 1927-28, their first season in the League.

During the close season Allen, together with team-mate Derek Hall, joined Swindon. It was a wise move. Allen played 40 times as the Robins swept to the Fourth Division title with a massive 102 points, eighteen ahead of their nearest rivals, Chester, while Torquay finished bottom again.

The following season, Allen lost his place to Fraser Digby, and in December 1986 returned to Torquay for a second spell, replacing the unfortunate John Smeulders. United were still in their customary position at the bottom of the table. Allen played in the remaining 28 games, including the final match of the season, when a draw with Crewe saw United escape the newly introduced relegation spot.

United's fortunes turned after this narrow escape. With Cyril Knowles in charge, they mounted a season-long promotion bid, only to fall short in the play-offs to Swansea. Allen was an ever present and was an able and reliable last line of defence. His height meant he could easily pluck balls out of the air and, for a tall man, he was agile.

Despite this, Allen was part of Knowles' summer cull and he rejoined Bath. Unfortunately, after nine games he broke his leg when conceding a penalty against Dorchester. He recovered by the following February, but was then deemed surplus to requirements and signed for Newport. His spell there was quickly aborted. The Welsh club's severe financial plight saw them fail to complete their Conference season.

Back at Plainmoor, new signing Ken Veysey had taken control of the No 1 jersey, but in a League match at Orient, suffered a season-ending injury. Youngster Mark Coombe deputised in the remaining league games but, unexpectedly, United had progressed to the Southern Area final of the Sherpa Van Trophy and Coombe was cup-tied. Allen again got the call and took his place between the sticks for the second leg at Molineux, which resulted in a famous 2-0 victory for the Gulls, having trailed 1-2 from the first leg.

Talk about fairy-tale endings. Seemingly on the soccer scrapheap and at the age of 37, Allen proudly marched out at Wembley for the final against Bolton. Well, perhaps it was not quite a fairy tale, as Bolton won 4-1. It proved to be Allen's final game for Torquay.

After football, Allen remained in south Devon, working for the Post Office. He is now an ambulance driver in the area, is a keen golfer and has played cricket for Chudleigh for many years.

Magic Moment: *During the Sherpa Van Southern Area final against Wolves, Allen pulled off a magnificent one-handed save that even had the Molineux faithful applauding.*

Worst Nightmare: *During the first leg of the 1988 play-off semi-final against Scunthorpe at Plainmoor, United were leading 2-0 when Allen dropped the ball, to allow Andy Flounders to grab a late and vital away goal.*

Torquay record	Appearances	Goals
League	132	0
FA Cup	5	0
League Cup	7	0

No 36. **MARK LORAM**

Debut: v Port Vale, 26 January 1985
Farewell: v Colchester, 4 September 1993

Mark Julian Loram was undoubtedly one of the most talented, some would argue *the* most talented player ever to don a Torquay United shirt. There is little doubt that, with the right attitude, he could have played at the highest level. But Loram was never one to seek fortune and fame. He loved a game of football, but equally enjoyed socialising with his friends in his home town.

Born in the fishing port of Brixham on 13 August 1967, Loram was an outstanding talent on the football pitch as a schoolboy, if not in the classroom itself. He played for Brixham Villa and quickly gained a reputation as a potential star of the future.

His upbringing was at times difficult. Away from football, he could be described as a loose cannon. Others may say he was just a typical teenager living in a small close-knit community. Those early years were not helped by the loss of friends in a deep-sea trawler accident.

The football grapevine went into overdrive, as other clubs were quickly alerted to this talent from South Devon, but Torquay were on the case and as far as Loram was concerned it was a no-brainer to join his local club.

Manager Dave Webb was soon drooling at the ability of the skinny, long-haired youngster. He had a mercurial left-foot and pace to boot. In training he was totally unfazed at being surrounded by battle-hardened old pros. Loram simply played as if it were a public park kickabout.

By the time Loram was handed his debut, Webb had little to lose. It was the end of January and Torquay had registered just four league victories, leaving them at the foot of the table. Veterans Eddie Kelly and Tony Currie had been introduced into the side, with Webb even picking himself on a couple of occasions. Loram was drafted into the attack and an away draw at mid-table Port Vale was almost tantamount to a shock result.

Loram found himself in and out of the side for the remainder of that season. United finished six points adrift at the bottom but, amid all the doom and gloom surrounding Plainmoor, was the realisation that United had a real talent on their hands. The question was: how long could they hold onto him?

The turbulence at Plainmoor continued into the next season. After just two games (and two defeats) Webb stepped down as manager to concentrate on his duties as managing director. Striker John Sims, who was now concentrating on his new duties as reserve-team coach, was handed the poison chalice, but with crowds dropping below the four-figure mark, and six defeats in seven games, he was quickly dispensed with.

Torquay's third manager of the season was Stuart Morgan, previously assistant to Harry Redknapp at Bournemouth. Results failed to improve, suggesting that it didn't really matter who was in charge, the quality of players just wasn't there. Loram was one of the few exceptions. Despite the dismal results, Morgan nurtured Loram, realising he would not respond to the hairdryer treatment, but preferred a kindly arm around the shoulder and a word or two of encouragement.

By Easter, United had yet again been cast adrift at the foot of the table and they bowed to the inevitable, allowing Loram to join QPR in a loan deal. That preceded a permanent move which was sealed in the summer, the fee being a paltry £15,000.

With hindsight, it could not have been a worse move. There was nothing wrong with QPR, managed by the wily Jim Smith, but the bright lights of the capital would prove too much of a distraction for the wide-eyed teenager.

Loram did not enjoy his time at Loftus Road at all. He didn't like the lodgings he was in, he missed his friends back home in Devon, and never felt as though he fitted in at the club. Despite this unhappiness, he still enjoyed his football. He was one of the outstanding players in Rangers' reserve side, to the extent that Smith considered picking him for a First Division debut against Liverpool. The problem was, Loram had gone AWOL, and not for the first time. In the end, he never did play a first-team game for Rangers as, in March 1987, with United in the all too familiar basement position, Morgan persuaded Smith to allow Loram to re-sign for the Gulls. Loram had little hesitation in accepting the move. It would be an exaggeration to say he had a profound impact on United's form, but his return gave a morale boost to the beleaguered supporters and his four goals in ten matches played a part in Morgan's side finishing one off the bottom to avoid relegation.

The close season saw the departure of Morgan to take charge of Weymouth. His replacement was former Spurs full-back Cyril Knowles, of 'Nice One Cyril' fame. Knowles' style of management was totally the opposite to Morgan's. He was a disciplinarian. He had played at the top level and expected dedication and professionalism, and some feared that Loram's relationship with his new boss would be put to the test. But Knowles new talent when he saw it. Yes, he gave Loram a few rollickings, but the duo showed respect for each other's qualities as well, and Loram rarely let Knowles down when it came to the nitty gritty of putting in a good shift on matchdays.

Knowles' first season saw Loram miss just one game as the Gulls' fortunes were transformed. They finished fifth, thus reaching the play-offs. The semi-final saw United take a narrow 2-1 lead to Scunthorpe for the second leg, but Loram's goal sealed a 1-1 draw and a two-legged final against Swansea, where they heartbreakingly lost 4-5 on aggregate.

The summer saw a regular input of new players, with some former favourites leaving. Loram suffered an early-season injury that kept him out until mid-October but he returned to again become an automatic choice. After the excitement of the previous season, league form was disappointing, with the lack of a regular goalscorer the main factor. The side finished mid-table, but saved its best performances for the cup competitions, reaching the third round of the FA Cup, losing 1-5 to First Division strugglers Sheffield Wednesday.

It was the much-maligned Sherpa Van Trophy that provided most of the memories, though. It was not a competition that stirred too many emotions or caused much interest, but try telling that to the United fans. The Gulls progressed fairly comfortably to the Southern Area final but were pitted against Wolves. By the very nature that they were in this particular competition, it is clear that that once-mighty club were now down among the also rans, but Wolves were still the overwhelming favourites. Wolves' 2-1 win at Plainmoor only confirmed that thought, but striker Dean Edwards scored at Molineux after just eight minutes. Then, two minutes before half-time, Loram's left foot again worked its magic, curling a sublime free-kick past Wolves' keeper Roger Hansbury from 25 yards. United survived the inevitable second-half bombardment to clinch an appearance at Wembley.

There was no fairy-tale ending. In front of a crowd of more than 46,000, Loram had a hand in United taking the lead, when his cross led to Edwards scoring. But Bolton came back strongly to win 4-1.

For Loram, the defeat had a nasty sting in its tail. The hot afternoon on the sapping Wembley turf took its toll and Loram felt unwell. Eventually he was diagnosed as being diabetic but, with the aid of medication, he was able to continue his career without any problems.

Historically, euphoria at Torquay's achievements doesn't last long and such was the case when, during the summer, Knowles made practically all his players available for transfer in an attempt to prune the wage bill, this despite a healthy return from the Wembley foray.

By the end of September, Knowles had resigned. United were struggling and were next to bottom, and his relationship with chairman Lew

Pope had been strained for some time. Despite yet another upset at the club, Loram continued to perform consistently, finishing as top scorer with thirteen. Results under new manager Dave Smith quickly improved, and United eventually finished in a comfortable fifteenth place.

Loram continued to thrill, excite and occasionally frustrate. The fans loved him. He had the occasional brush with the law. Nothing serious, usually just the result of a drink or two too many.

Of course, there was another Wembley appearance, when Loram was part of the side that triumphed over Blackpool in the Division Four play-off final in May 1991.

Loram gradually faded from the scene. He had brief loan spells at Stockport and Exeter, but was brought back to Torquay in 1993 on a non-contract basis, when he made a brief final cameo appearance as a substitute at home to Colchester.

He joined Minehead and later played for various teams around the south Devon area, playing into his 40s. That, in itself, must silence those who said he had wasted his talent and did not love the game enough. He did love playing football, but made the game look so easy at times that he often gave the impression of not trying.

Magic Moment: *Loram scored an incredible goal at Burnley in April 1987. He collected the ball in his own half, flicked the ball over one opponent, beat another and sent a left-foot (of course) shot screaming into the top corner.*

Worst Nightmare: *In the Division Four play-off final at Wembley in May 1991, Loram was the only Torquay player to miss a penalty in the shoot-out after the scores had been tied 2-2 after extra-time.*

TORQUAY RECORD	Appearance	Goals
League	263	48
FA Cup	19	8
League Cup	17	1

No 37. **TOM KELLY**

Debut: v Burnley, 23 August 1986
Farewell: v Scunthorpe, 6 April 1996

As is the case with a number of players, Thomas John Kelly had two separate spells with Torquay, giving solid service to the club during both.

Kelly was born in Bellshill, near Motherwell, in Scotland on 28 March
1964. At seventeen he joined Hibernian from non-league side Gartcosh
United, but after two years at the Edinburgh club was released, subsequently joining Partick Thistle and then Queen of the South.

In August 1985, he journeyed south, joining Hartlepool on a free
transfer with the hope of some first-team action. Although never able to
get an extended run in the side, he played fifteen games in that first season but, disappointingly for him, was released again.

In the summer of 1986, Torquay boss Stuart Morgan was having a
hectic time wheeling and dealing. After two successive seasons of finishing at the bottom of the pack, it was clear that the United squad needed
much strengthening, and among the number of new arrivals were Kelly
and his Hartlepool team-mate, Paul Dobson.

Although hoping for a fresh start, Kelly was again frustratingly in and
out of the side, but after a 3-5 home defeat by Swansea in late October,
he was one of a number of changes made by Morgan, and had an extended spell on the left-hand side of midfield.

United's form didn't improve, but when full-back Phil King was transferred to Swindon in January, the left-footed Kelly was a natural replacement at left-back.

The switch of position seemed to suit Kelly. He was quick, a tenacious
tackler, and liked to get forward. After their early-season benevolence, the
United defence tightened up but the season was still a struggle, culminating in the final day 'great escape' match against Crewe.

With Cyril Knowles installed as the new manager, United were a different animal for the new campaign. Knowles took the fear of out of losing, encouraging a more attacking style, employing three central defenders, so allowing Kelly and fellow full-back Jim McNichol to break forward
at every opportunity. Kelly thrived on these tactics, his energetic style
coming to the fore as United eventually succumbed to Swansea in the
play-offs. The fans were impressed, too, as Kelly was their choice for
'Player of the Year'.

In 1988-89, Kelly was again a model of consistency, missing just two
games and playing his part in United's Sherpa Van Trophy final defeat by

Bolton at Wembley. He then found himself transferred to York as Knowles was forced to drastically trim his squad during the summer, with United's bank manager again having sleepless nights over the state of the club's finances.

Kelly was straight into the team at York, but his stay in Yorkshire was brief, with his wife unable to settle in the area. He therefore jumped at the opportunity to make a quick return to Devon when Exeter made a successful transfer deadline bid of £15,000.

Kelly won a Fourth Division winners' medal with the Grecians in 1990, and played 88 league games for them, scoring nine times.

In January 1993, Kelly returned for his second spell at Plainmoor on a free transfer. With Paul Compton in the hot seat, United had struggled to string results together. Neil Warnock was brought in as a management consultant and quickly moved to strengthen certain areas of the team, particularly left-back, which had been a problem position for most of the season.

Kelly was as dependable as ever and took over penalty-taking duties. Under Warnock, United's results improved sufficiently to avoid relegation.

The following season saw Kelly revert mainly to his old midfield role as United battled their way into the play-offs, losing a feisty two-legged encounter with Preston.

Kelly remained an almost permanent fixture in the United line up, but was one of a number of players left out after the 1-8 home drubbing by Scunthorpe that would cost manager Don O'Riordan his job. He was soon back in the fold but, with United finishing in last place and being saved by the inadequacies of the Stevenage ground, he was one of a number of players released by Eddie May at the end of the season.

After that, Kelly played for a number of non-league clubs in the South West, including Weymouth, Teignmouth and Ilfracombe, before moving to Taunton, where he was appointed captain by former United team-mate Russell Musker. Kelly eventually took on a player-coach role and played in Taunton's FA Vase final victory over Berkhamstead Town at Villa Park in 2001.

After further spells at Bideford and Bridgwater where he required a cartilage operation, he plied his trade at a number of clubs in south Devon. In September 2009 he was appointed as manager of local side Bovey Tracey and he still plays at the age of 45, alongside his son, Cameron.

Magic Moment: *Kelly finally scored his first goal for United in his 144th league and cup game for the club. Fittingly it was the only goal of the game against his former team, York.*

Worst Nightmare: *In the penultimate game of the 1987-88 season, United needed a win at Burnley to make automatic promotion a near certainty, but Kelly's ill-judged back-pass to keeper Kenny Allen allowed the Clarets to score the only goal of the game.*

TORQUAY RECORD	Appearances	Goals
League	237	8
FA Cup	15	0
League Cup	15	0

No 38. JIM McNICHOL

Debut: v Burnley, 23 August 1986
Farewell: v Hull, 21 September 1991

'Please don't ask him about the dog, everyone else does.' That was the opening gambit from Jim McNichol's mother-in-law, when your author phoned to speak to him. I promised I wouldn't, as the infamous incident that leaves McNichol's name permanently etched in Torquay United folklore is documented enough elsewhere. We cannot, of course, leave the incident unmentioned and we will come to that later.

James Anthony McNichol was born in Glasgow on 9 June 1958 but began his football career as an apprentice at Ipswich. In July 1976 he joined Luton as a professional, playing intermittently in the two seasons he spent at Kenilworth Road.

A transfer fee of £30,000 took him to Brentford in October 1978, where he soon established a regular spot in the heart of the Bees' defence. The home supporters quickly took to him, not just for his cool and effective defending but for his ability to fire in long-range shots from both open play and free-kicks.

If a free-kick was awarded within 40 yards of goal, the cry of 'Jimeeeee, Jimeeeee' would inevitably strike up from the Griffin Park terraces. McNichol was reasonably successful as well, as his record of 22 goals from 151 league starts suggests. Seven Scottish Under-21 caps also came his way.

The Bees' fans were upset when McNichol departed for Exeter in July 1984. His central defensive partnership with former Torquay player, Pat Kruse, was reckoned by many Brentford regulars to be one of the best in the club's history. To rub salt into the wounds, McNichol left on a free transfer.

McNichol's debut for Exeter resulted in a 5-0 win over Northampton, but it was a result that flattered to deceive. The Grecians struggled for much of the season. McNichol was one of sixteen newcomers to the squad and one of the few successes. As well as the indifferent league form, City were knocked out of the FA Cup by non-league Enfield. Following that defeat, McNichol was handed the captaincy. With four games to go, manager Jim Iley was asked to resign. He refused, and was duly sacked as City finished a lowly eighteenth in Division Four.

Under new manager Colin Appleton, City fared even worse, finishing 21st. Again, McNichol was one of the few to perform consistently but, surprisingly, at the end of the season he was only offered a three-month contract.

McNichol had just taken over a pub in Ashburton, and manager Appleton believed the new venture would prove a distraction. At Plainmoor, manager Stuart Morgan jumped at the chance to bring McNichol in after a disastrous previous season in which United had finished bottom of the League. Under new rules, the team suffering that fate for the new campaign would be relegated to the Conference.

McNichol was one of a number of new recruits, including fellow Exeter team-mates Phil King and John Impey. King did not stay long, moving to Swindon after 24 games, which upset Exeter, who were due an additional payment when the full-back had played 25 games!

The season started reasonably well. Two defeats in the first ten games did little to suggest that a relegation scrap was on the cards, but that was how it turned out after a terrible string of results. Going into the final game of the season, the relegation battle was between three teams. United sat on 47 points. Burnley were below them on 46, and Lincoln above them on 48. Given the poor form of the respective opponents, United's task looked the easiest as they went into the home game with Crewe.

No one could foretell the drama that was to unfold. An understandably nervous Torquay conceded two goals in five minutes just before half-time. In the second half, United pulled one back, but with the clock ticking and Burnley ahead in their game, the Gulls looked doomed.

Cue a certain police Alsatian named Bryn. As full-time approached, police moved to the perimeter of the pitch to prevent a pitch invasion.

Bryn's handler was watching the crowd. Bryn was not. McNichol, playing at right-back, rushed to collect the ball but Bryn, believing his handler was about to be attacked, sank his teeth into McNichol's thigh.

McNichol clearly needed treatment which took several minutes to administer. He later required a dozen stitches in the wound. In the ensuing impasse, news filtered through that Lincoln were two goals down at Swansea. With a superior goal-difference, a draw would be enough to save Torquay. Sure enough, in the fourth minute of stoppage time, striker Paul Dobson fired home and United were saved. Bryn was hailed the hero, although even his mighty molars did not deter several hundred joyous fans who streamed onto the pitch at the final whistle to hoist their heroes shoulder high.

The incident made national headlines with the usual 'doggy' related corny headlines.

With Cyril Knowles installed as the new manager for the 1987-88 season, United adopted a new system of play, utilising a five-man defence, with McNichol at right-back and Tom Kelly his opposite number encouraged to push forward. It was testimony to McNichol's all-round ability. He was strong in the air but, for a big man, comfortable and skilful on the ball.

The tactics suited McNichol. Never afraid to have a pot shot, he scored nine times in a season when he wore the No 2 shirt in every game, including three in the two unsuccessful play-off matches against Swansea.

The following season again saw McNichol as a regular. The League campaign was a disappointment, after the near miss of the previous year, but McNichol proudly led his team out as captain at Wembley for the Sherpa Van Trophy final against Bolton, which United lost 1-4.

From Wembley to the transfer list. In an effort to reduce the wage bill, Knowles put everyone up for sale during the summer and McNichol was one of the departees, returning to Exeter on a free transfer.

City, now managed by Terry Cooper, had not pulled up any trees since McNichol's first spell there, but suddenly things clicked into place. City stormed to the Fourth Division title with McNichol scoring eight league goals, including an unlikely hat-trick against Rochdale.

McNichol appeared in just eleven City games in Division Three before leaving to concentrate on his pub business. He was briefly brought back by United in September 1991, playing two games before calling it a day, playing later for Torrington.

To this day, he remains the landlord of the Exeter Inn at Ashburton, and is also a single-figure handicap golfer. He is always happy to chat about his football days – just try not to mention the dog too often!

Magic Moment: *It is often forgotten that during the 'Bryn the Dog' game, it was McNichol's 47th-minute deflected free-kick that put United back in the game.*

Worst Nightmare: *In March 1985, McNichol played at the heart of the Exeter defence when the Grecians suffered a 1-7 defeat and a 1-5 loss in the space of five days.*

TORQUAY RECORD	Appearances	Goals
League	126	13
FA Cup	9	1
League Cup	8	0

No 39. PHIL LLOYD

Debut: Wrexham, 15 August 1987
Farewell: v Wigan, 7 March 1992

One look at Phil Lloyd's Torquay statistics probably says it all. He joined Torquay in the summer of 1987 and did not miss a match in his first season, or his second, or his third. Every league and cup match, the moustachioed Lloyd was there. He did even not drop out of a Sherpa Van/Leyland DAF Trophy game, a competition which generally gives managers an excuse to rest key players at times.

Lloyd was simply too valuable to the team. A rock-solid central defender, he would come under the hard-but-fair category. By the end of 90 minutes, his opponent knew they had been in a game.

Perhaps it is not surprising that Philip Rowan Lloyd was as tough as teak. He was born in the middle of a Yorkshire winter, at Hemsworth, on Boxing Day 1964, to be precise. He joined Middlesbrough as an apprentice, turning professional when he was eighteen, but was released the following year without getting a sniff of a first-team appearance and joined Barnsley on a non-contract basis.

Again, a first-team opportunity eluded him, but in March 1984 he got his chance at Darlington. The club had emerged from a dire financial crisis two years earlier, which they survived thanks in part to the local community, which organised various fund-raising activities.

The manager was a certain Cyril Knowles, who achieved minor miracles at Darlington, taking the club from the brink of extinction to promotion to Division Three at the end of the 1984-85 season. Lloyd proved to be an integral part of that success, being one of the mainstays in a mean defence.

The following season, 'Darlo' reached the heady heights of thirteenth place in Division Three, their best finish since the new four-division League structure was introduced in 1958. The following year they were relegated, prompting Knowles' departure.

When Knowles was appointed Torquay manager in the summer of 1987, he must have felt a touch of *déjà vu*. Again, he was asked to rescue an ailing club from the lower reaches of the League.

Knowles soon set about strengthening his squad and turned again to Lloyd. His reliable centre-half had played over 130 games for him at Darlington in four seasons and the new Gulls' boss knew he was getting an ultra-reliable defender who he could build the foundations of a new team around.

Lloyd was immediately employed as part of a three-man central defensive unit, alongside David Cole and John Impey. Clearly Knowles' first intention was to stop conceding goals, so even he was stunned when United won their opening game of the season 6-1 against Wrexham.

Knowles again showed he had the Midas touch by leading the Gulls to the play-offs, with Cole joining Lloyd with an ever-present record.

1988-89 saw Lloyd embark on what was, for him, a prolific scoring streak. By the end of October he had notched four goals. He would score just once more for the season but what a vital goal it was, being the only strike in the Sherpa Van Trophy Southern semi final at Brentford.

The run in during that competition provided one of the highlights of Lloyd's career, and his performance in the semi-final second-leg win at Molineux, when he kept the prolific Steve Bull quiet, was vital in getting United to Wembley.

The following year saw Lloyd win United's 'Player of the Year' title, with the fans recognising his consistency in what was a disappointing season overall. The following started more promisingly, but ended badly for Lloyd when he suffered a serious injury that would keep him out for a year (see Worst Nightmare). He missed United's Wembley play-off triumph over Blackpool, and after a long battle to regain fitness, he finally regained his first-team place, earning a massive reception from the fans on his comeback against Preston in December 1991.

Nevertheless, the injury had taken its toll. Lloyd managed only another twelve games for the club.

After leaving Plainmoor, Lloyd played for Dorchester, Dawlish and Elmore before he had a spell managing Barnstaple. In recent years he has been a regular visitor to the Plainmoor press box as a match analyst.

Magic Moment: *Lloyd's fourth game for Torquay took him back to Darlington, where he received a great reception from the appreciative home supporters.*

Worst Nightmare: *Lloyd's long unbroken run of appearances was ended when he suffered a broken leg at Maidstone three days before Christmas 1990.*

TORQUAY RECORD	Appearances	Goals
League	170	7
FA Cup	14	1
League Cup	12	0

No 40. **LEE SHARPE**

Debut: v Exeter, 3 October 1987
Farewell: v Swansea (play-offs), 28 May 1988

Lee Stuart Sharpe, born on 27 May 1971, only had a brief Plainmoor career, but despite the fact that he was born in Halesowen in the West Midlands, is regarded by the Torquay faithful as the local boy made good. Certainly, no other ex-Gull has gone on to greater fame, or fortune, come to that.

As a youngster, Sharpe was football mad. As with thousands of other boys of a similar age, he set his mind on becoming a professional footballer, to the extent that this was largely all he thought about and he left school without any qualifications.

He played for Stourbridge Falcons, a club that consistently produced some of the best youth sides in the Midlands, and the young Sharpe quickly gained a reputation as a skilful and dangerous player.

When he was fifteen, he was spotted by a Birmingham scout and, despite being an Aston Villa fan, jumped at the chance to sign for the Blues as a schoolboy. But Sharpe did not enjoy the experience and was eventually released, being told that he had the skill but not the aggression.

A couple of days later, he was invited to Torquay for a three-day trial. By his own admission it was a tortuous experience, as he played three full games in that time, including an outing for the first-team in a Devon Professional Bowl match against Exeter.

But Gulls boss Stuart Morgan was impressed by Sharpe's raw talent, his ability to run at and beat defenders, and he had a strong left foot. Sharpe boarded the train back to Birmingham with the offer of a two-year apprenticeship. He also had a trial with West Brom and the chance of a trial with Wolves, but United's was a concrete offer and he soon signed.

Sharpe headed south for the start of the 1987-88 season, but quickly realised whilst the title of 'apprentice with Torquay' may have impressed some of the local girls, the reality was very different. He was away from home for the first time, shacked up in 'digs' with a couple of other apprentices, and spent his first week attempting to spruce up Plainmoor ready for the new season.

During the summer, Morgan had been sacked, with Cyril Knowles taking over. Knowles kept faith with the new boys and handed them over to youth-team coaches Sean Haselgrave and Derek 'The Dude' Dawkins. The duo put the apprentices through a murderous and disciplined training regime, but it sorted the men from the boys.

Sharpe was soon handed a first-team chance. He had been sent home for a week, the coaches realising he was homesick, but within a couple of days, was asked to return as cover for injuries. He found himself sitting on the bench for the local derby at home to Exeter. With 25 minutes remaining, he was sent on for his debut. He was only sixteen.

Sharpe's involvement with the first team became more regular. He would often travel away with them as an extra body, and occasionally sit on the bench, but the tough training regime was working and he was improving all the time.

Despite the fact that United were still in a promotion battle, Knowles showed great faith in the youngster's ability and, with just eleven games of the season remaining, thrust Sharpe back into the side. He did not let his manager down. He had the confidence to take, and score, a penalty against Cardiff.

The next game was a Friday night home fixture against Colchester. It was a turgid, forgettable game, but it would be a night that Sharpe would remember for the rest of his life. It was the night that he was told Manchester United wanted to sign him.

A scout had seen him and tipped off United manager Alex Ferguson, who had watched his display against Colchester and seen enough. It was the ultimate testimony to Sharpe's natural ability.

Understandably, Sharpe wasted little time in agreeing a deal. Torquay were happy too. The fee of £180,000, rising to £300,000, was a fortune.

The agreement was that Sharpe would remain at Plainmoor until the end of the season. Word soon spread about this boy wonder, and Knowles protected him by only using him in home games, thus sheltering him from the hostilities of other club's supporters.

If Sharpe's rise to first-team status was impressively quick at Torquay, it was matched at Old Trafford. Ferguson, never afraid to blood youngsters if he believes they are good enough, soon brought Sharpe into the first-team fold, initially in the unfamiliar role of left-back. Sharpe quickly adapted. He was quick, strong and could tackle as well, ideal attributes for the position. Eventually, with the transfer of Ralph Milne, Sharpe was restored to his left-wing role.

Belying his age and inexperience, Sharpe soon became one of the most talked about players in the country. He was exciting to watch, the type who would lift a crowd whenever he received the ball. Honours soon came his way. In 1990-91, he was voted the PFA Young Player of the Year, won a European Cup-Winners' Cup medal, and had also scored a stunning hat-trick in a 6-2 League Cup thrashing of Arsenal. He won eight England Under-21 caps and received a call up to the full squad as understudy to John Barnes, eventually making his debut at the tender age of nineteen.

Behind the scenes, Ferguson was having concerns about the lifestyle of some of his younger players, Sharpe included. Much of it was the normal high jinks that any highly paid young man would indulge in. Sharpe was then struck down with an illness that would keep him out for a lengthy period. It was diagnosed as viral meningitis.

He eventually recovered but now faced competition for his left-wing slot from Ryan Giggs. There was still time for Sharpe to score with a cheeky backheel against Barcelona in the Champions League.

Other injuries began to take their toll as well, and his Old Trafford career was now slowly in decline. In the end, he was deemed surplus to requirements, having made 265 appearances, scoring 36 goals and won eight full England caps. Despite his injury record, Leeds gambled on paying £4.5 million for him. It was a gamble that did not pay off. Sharpe missed the entire 1997-98 season with a knee injury, and ended up playing just 30 games for Leeds.

To aid his recovery, he was loaned to Italian side Sampdoria but played only three games. A further loan spell at Bradford was more successful, and Leeds eventually agreed to sell him to their Yorkshire neighbours for a knock-down £250,000. He helped City to promotion to the Premiership but again fell out of favour. From then on his career drifted to a conclusion with brief spells at Portsmouth, Exeter and Icelandic side Grindavik, before announcing his retirement at the age of 32.

Sharpe made a brief return with Kidderminster Sunday League side Hoobrook Crown and non-league Garforth, but by this time a media and TV career was beginning to take off. Sharpe has been a pundit on *Match of the Day* and *Football Focus*, as well as appearing in reality TV shows such as *Dancing on Ice* and *Celebrity Love Island*. He also features regularly as an after-dinner speaker.

Magic Moment: *Sharpe was dragged out of bed at one o'clock in the morning to be told that Manchester United wanted to sign him.*

Worst Nightmare: *Sharpe was subjected to constant media pressure during his absence with viral meningitis. Rumours abounded that he was suffering from a drugs related problem.*

Torquay record	Appearances	Goals
League	17	3
FA Cup	0	0
League Cup	0	0

No 41. **DAVE CALDWELL**

Debut: v Stockport, 6 November 1987
Farewell: v Exeter, 14 April 1990

It is difficult to do justice to David Wilson Caldwell's career in a short profile such as this. He was undoubtedly one of the most colourful characters to have plied his trade in the Football League and, despite a relatively small number of appearances for Torquay, he quickly achieved cult hero status as, indeed, he did at two of his other clubs.

Born in Aberdeen on 31 July 1960, Caldwell had football in his blood. His father, also David, was a stalwart defender for Aberdeen in the 1950s. Dave junior, however, was a striker from the outset. He recalls scoring 130 goals in a season whilst at primary school but, after being intellectually good enough to attend grammar school, it was to his dismay that he discovered the school did not play football and he was forced to chose between rugby and hockey. Caldwell continued to play football in the local leagues, however, and was top scorer in the Under-15 league in Aberdeen.

His rise into the professional ranks was fairly rapid. He signed for Inverness Caledonian, then a Highland League side and, after scoring thirteen goals in as many games, was signed by Mansfield for £25,000 in June 1979.

He had to be patient at Field Mill. He was given his debut as a substitute in a defeat at Reading in September of that year, but had to wait until the following April for his full debut. His apprentice in those early days was Colin Calderwood, a future Scottish international. The speedy Caldwell takes credit for teaching Calderwood how to run properly. 'He was flat-footed and had no speed before I showed him what to do,' recalls Caldwell.

The following season saw him the start in impressive fashion. In the first game of the season he scored an 89th-minute equaliser in a League Cup-tie at Doncaster, when he collected a long clearance near halfway, beat several defenders and crashed the ball home. It was the first of many spectacular goals during his career, none better than in a second round FA Cup-tie against non-league Mossley. Winning the ball well into his own half, Caldwell proceeded to waltz past several hapless defenders, wriggled his way along the bye-line, and fired a left-foot shot into the top corner. It was, by his own admission, the best goal of his career.

By early February the free-scoring Mansfield side were turning into promotion candidates, but a poor run saw them miss out on promotion, costing manager Mick Jones his job. For Caldwell, there was the first of many suspensions, when he racked up a string of bookings. Later in the season he was sent off at Scunthorpe for kicking an opponent who was lying on the ground after being fouled by him.

Caldwell's hot-headedness on the field strangely endeared him to the home support. His exciting, fearless play and spectacular goals helped. Had he been mediocre, no doubt the crowd would have turned against him for his regular indiscipline, but he was Mansfield's loveable rogue and, conversely, loathed by opposition fans.

Caldwell's Mansfield career continued to ebb and flow. Barren spells were followed by a run of goals. There was the occasional tap in, but mostly they were stunning solo efforts or long-range shots. Had the Stags been a First Division side with their games on *Match of the Day* each week, Caldwell might have monopolised the 'Goal of the Season' competition.

In September 1982, Caldwell was disgruntled with life at Field Mill and requested a transfer, saying that club was going nowhere. Within a fortnight he had retracted both his request and his comments.

The 1983-84 season was interesting, even by Caldwell's standards. After an arrest for drink driving, he walked out of Ilkeston Magistrates Court before his case could be heard, as he feared he would miss the team bus to Huddersfield. On his return home from the match he was rear-rested. He was later banned from driving for a year and fined £120, which he was allowed to repay at £20 per week, as he successfully convinced the court that his earnings were less than the average working man!

At the beginning of October he scored his first hat-trick, at home to Aldershot, but Caldwell finished the game believing he had scored four, not realising that another effort had been disallowed.

He soon turned from hero to villain again. In October, at Reading he was lectured after one minute for a spat with a Royals defender. After fourteen minutes he was back in the dressing room, sent off after aiming a punch at formidable central defender Martin Hicks. The match ended in 0-4 defeat for Mansfield, prompting manager Ian Greaves to place Caldwell on the transfer list for failing to curb his disciplinary problems.

Caldwell's response was typical. Four days later he scored four times in a 5-0 win over Hartlepool, although Greaves remained unrepentant. Caldwell finished the season with 23 goals and also earned himself a new contract.

Caldwell started the 1984-85 season in good form, but a week after scoring eleven seconds into an FA Cup match against Rotherham, he handed in another transfer request, this time saying that he needed a fresh challenge.

A few days before Christmas, he went to Carlisle on loan, vowing that if he had not sorted out a new club by 29 December, he would give up football and return to Scotland. He remained at Carlisle for two months but did not enjoy the experience. He picked up an injury, and the saving grace was the regular drinking sessions with team-mate Ian Bishop, the future West Ham and Manchester City midfielder.

After returning to Mansfield, Caldwell went on loan to Swindon. Manager Lou Macari played him in a role behind the two strikers, but Swindon's finances wouldn't stretch to a permanent transfer and it was back to Mansfield.

At the end of the season, Caldwell was transferred to Chesterfield for £12,000. The fans were desperately sorry to see him leave. Despite his ups and downs, there was never a dull moment. He left Field Mill with a record of 66 goals in 188 games, 36 bookings, two dismissals and eight suspensions.

It was much the same story at Chesterfield – spectacular goals and disciplinary problems. Caldwell tells the story of how he was sent off after just four minutes – for persistent misconduct! On another occasion he was dismissed for a two-footed lunge on an opponent. Unfortunately, the ball was about 50 yards away.

In October 1987, Chesterfield decided he could leave. He had already been sent off twice that season. Caldwell was told to expect a phone call from Cyril Knowles, who was interested in signing him. Caldwell thought Knowles was managing Darlington, and that was not a move he fancied, so he was somewhat surprised to be told that he was travelling to Torquay for talks.

Caldwell duly travelled to Devon and was put up at the Livermead Cliff Hotel. On a beautiful day, he and Knowles held talks on the balcony. Knowles waxed lyrical about the beauty of the area, his ambitions for the club, and how wonderful the night life was. The latter particularly appealed to Caldwell, who also managed to secure a pay rise, and the contract was signed there and then.

With the ink barely dry, Knowles then delivered his ultimatum. If Caldwell was seen drinking, or in a nightclub, he would be fined two weeks' wages. Caldwell felt slightly aggrieved but, these days, on reflection, he names Knowles as the best manager he played under, believing that if he had a disciplinarian manager early in his career, he would not have had the problems he did.

Caldwell soon endeared himself to the Plainmoor faithful, scoring the only goal of the game with an overhead kick on his home debut against Hereford. The next match he was sent off. He would be dismissed on a further two occasions that season. Naturally, the FA were not too enamoured with this record, and he was summoned to appear at Lancaster Gate, but the Christmas period intervened and the hearing postponed. It was rearranged and due to be held in Bristol, but United were in the running for promotion and desperate to have Caldwell available. In the knowledge that the FA would throw the book at their striker and that he faced a long suspension, a mysterious medical note appeared, stating that Caldwell was unfit to make the marathon journey to Bristol. Admirably, United managed to drag the whole affair out until the end of the season when Caldwell was handed an eight-game ban.

Having lost in the two-legged play-off final to Swansea, Caldwell left for foreign shores, joining Belgian side KVV Overpelt for £13,000. It was, by his own admission, the worst thing he did. He managed to avoid his ban by moving abroad but it was not an experience Caldwell enjoyed, not helped by a broken ankle during his spell there.

In December 1989, he returned to Torquay on loan and stayed until the end of the season, scoring six times. As was the case at both Mansfield and Chesterfield, the Torquay fans adored Caldwell. He was an entertainer but could also play a bit. He was quick, skilful and a fine leader of the line.

It was then off to South Africa. Caldwell loved the lifestyle there, even though the standard of football he was playing in was not particularly impressive. He remained for eighteen months, but returned for a second spell at Chesterfield, with Overpelt receiving £14,500, having retained his registration.

In May 1992, he returned to Scotland after a cartilage injury forced his retirement from League football. He again joined Inverness Caledonian and later managed Highland League side Lossiemouth, but off the field, Caldwell's life was in a mess. He was drinking heavily and had no job. Fortunately, he was offered a job selling photocopiers, although he admits with typical humour that he was not sure what a photocopier was.

To his credit, his life got back together. He progressed within the company and still works for them today, based in Glasgow.

He admits that his time at Torquay was the most enjoyable of his career. Despite his hero status elsewhere, it is the only club he has returned to since retiring, and was overwhelmed with the reception he received when introduced to the Plainmoor crowd when attending a match in April 2009.

Those who ever saw Caldwell play will surely remember the experience. There was usually a wonder goal, regular disagreements with the officials, or a fracas with an opponent, not to mention the bleached blond 'mullett'. On occasions he would look unfit, lazy and uninterested, and then burst into life with a marvellous piece of skill.

The 30-minute phone conversation with him was one of the funniest half-hours your author has spent. Twenty years on, Dave Caldwell is still just as entertaining.

Magic Moment: *In a poll conducted by* FourFourTwo Magazine, *Mansfield supporters voted Caldwell as the club's greatest ever player. He was not aware of the accolade until it was mentioned to him by your author.*

Worst Nightmare: *Caldwell's five dismissals in the 1987-88 season constitutes an unwanted Football League record.*

TORQUAY RECORD	Appearances	Goals
League	41	10
FA Cup	4	1
League Cup	0	0

No 42. **MATT ELLIOTT**

Debut: v Stockport, 31 March 1989
Farewell: v Leyton Orient, 21 March 1992

Like Lee Sharpe before him, Matthew Stephen Elliott won international honours and became a £1 million-plus player in his post-Torquay career. That is where the similarity ends, though. Elliott was a muscular, powerful central defender.

Born in Epsom on 1 November 1968, Elliott soon cut an imposing figure in his teens, making him a dominant figure in youth football. On leaving school, he worked as a labourer and played part-time for non-league sides Leatherhead and Epsom & Ewell.

In 1988, he was picked up by Charlton for £5,000 after a successful trial, but he made just one League Cup appearance for the Addicks. He was brought to Torquay by Cyril Knowles just prior to deadline day in March 1989 for a fee of £10,000.

The remainder of that season saw Elliott enjoy mixed fortunes. He quickly settled into the rigours of Fourth Division football but ended up on the winning side just three times in the league. In contrast, Torquay were enjoying a golden run in the Sherpa Van Trophy, a competition that barely captivated the imagination of the paying spectators but at least had the promise of a Wembley appearance for the finalists.

United had cruised through five rounds, conceding just one goal, but were due to meet Wolves in the two-legged Southern final. The Midlanders had crushed virtually everyone they had played throughout the season, with the potent strike-force of Steve Bull and Andy Mutch scoring for fun.

Plainmoor hosted the first game. Elliott had a hand in setting up United's goal, scored by Dean Edwards, and the big defender also kept Bull quiet – until the last ten minutes, when the striker, who shortly after would feature in the England team, scored twice.

The tie seemed beyond reach but, in the second leg, a crowd of over 22,000 were silenced as United sealed their Wembley place with a 2-0 win – one of the shock results of the season.

The final didn't go to plan – losing 1-4 to Bolton – but for Elliott it had been a thrilling experience so soon into his career.

Elliott became the lynchpin of the Torquay defence. At 6ft 3ins, he was dominant in the air and a constant menace at set-pieces. He relished the physical challenges and his occasional over-zealousness sometimes landed him in trouble with officialdom.

In 1990-91, he was back at Wembley, this time tasting success with United defeating Blackpool in the Fourth Division play-off final.

The 1992-93 season was to be Elliott's last as a Gull. United were struggling and, prior to the transfer deadline, Elliott moved to Fourth Division Scunthorpe, initially on a loan deal. Many had predicted greater things for him, but the move down a division seemed to signal a career of mediocrity. That would not be the case.

The Iron were impressed enough to pay Torquay £50,000 to make the arrangement permanent. Elliott went from strength to strength, and within eighteen months was on the move again, this time to Oxford, his fee having increased to £150,000.

He remained at Oxford for just over three years, helping them to promotion to Division One in 1995-96. Elliott improved massively as a player and his dominant performances were being watched at close quarters by a number of clubs. It was Leicester, managed by Martin O'Neill, who finally won the battle to sign him, paying £1,600,000, easily a record for both clubs.

The thought of facing Premier League strikers week in, week out, was one that Elliott relished. His fitness improved no end, but the desire and will to win was a quality O'Neill admired in a player, and Elliott certainly possessed that. The close-shaved head also added to the imposing look.

Leicester were by now an established mid-table Premiership side with ambition. Elliott was made captain and continued to earn rave reviews. Eventually, international honours came his way. His grandmother was Scottish, making him eligible to play for that country. Craig Brown selected him for the Scottish squad and he made his international debut as a substitute against France in November 1997, the first of eighteen caps, scoring once.

Elliott was also selected for the Scotland World Cup squad that reached the finals in France in 1998, although he was not picked for any for the group games, at which stage Scotland were eliminated.

In 1999-2000, Elliott led Leicester to arguably their best ever season, finishing eighth in the Premiership and winning the League Cup final, thus ensuring European football.

When O'Neill left to manage Celtic, he began to raid Leicester for their best players. Neil Lennon and Steve Guppy had already gone north, but a £3.5 million bid for Elliott was turned down.

The Foxes' fans were mightily relieved. Elliott by now had become a cult hero during the final days of the old Filbert Street stadium. Indeed, when the club moved to the new Walkers Stadium, Elliott was the first captain to lead the side out there.

After the highs at Leicester, inevitably there were lows as well. After O'Neill's departure, things were not quite the same. City were relegated in 2001-02 and Elliott became embroiled in the scandal that enveloped the club on a mid-season break to La Manga in 2004, when nine players were arrested after allegations by three German tourists of sexual assault. Elliott was not accused of assault, but of breaking and entering, and failing to assist the women. He was held by police overnight but cleared of any involvement, but it was still a chastening experience.

Injuries were now playing an increasing role in Elliott's career. After a three-month lay-off, he was left out of the side by Micky Adams and it was the beginning of the end of his career. A loan spell at Ipswich followed, but in 2005 he called it a day, a persistent knee injury finally ending a career spanning over 700 games.

Since then, Elliott has run a shop in Oxford, overseen coaching courses with former Leicester team-mate Gerry Taggart, and more recently teamed up again with ex-Torquay colleague Dean Edwards as the managerial duo at Hednesford Town. He is also still involved at Leicester as one of the community coaches.

Magic Moment: *Elliott scored both Leicester goals as they beat Tranmere 2-1 at Wembley to win the League Cup in 2000.*

Worst Nightmare: *Elliott suffered the ignominy of being sent off whilst playing for his country against the Faroe Islands.*

TORQUAY RECORD	Appearances	Goals
League	124	15
FA Cup	9	2
League Cup	9	2

No 43. **WES SAUNDERS**

Debut: v Walsall, 25 August 1990
Farewell: v Rochdale, 20 March 1993

Wesley Saunders was in the mould of Matt Elliott – a strong and powerful player. He also happens to be Elliott's brother-in-law, as well as also being related to another former Torquay player – Micky Holmes.

Saunders was born in Boldon, Tyne and Wear, on 23 February 1963. An outstanding schoolboy player at his school, Boldon Comprehensive, he was snapped up as a junior by Newcastle and rose through the ranks to turn professional in June 1981 and was given his first-team debut in November of that year in an away match against Chelsea.

Saunders began to make the left-back position his own and made steady progress. His no-nonsense approach to the game endeared him to the Toon Army, if not always to the match officials.

He made 79 League appearances for Newcastle, but by the mid-1980s found himself on the sidelines more frequently. His cause was not helped by the fact that he was part of the Magpies' defence in a bizarre 5-5 draw against QPR in September 1984. United were four up by half-time, but totally capitulated in the second half, leaving manager Jack Charlton even more exasperated than usual.

In March 1985, Saunders had a brief loan spell at Bradford City and, in August of that year, moved to Carlisle for a fee of £20,000. His top-flight experience made him an automatic choice and he notched up over 100 appearances. It also made him one of the higher earners at Brunton Park, and when Carlisle found themselves needing to make financial cutbacks, Saunders was one of the players shown the door.

A spell in Scotland with Dundee followed but, in July 1990, Torquay manager Dave Smith, backed by the new chairman, Mike Bateson, splashed out a club record £60,000 to make Saunders a Gull. Saunders was one of four debutants in the opening game of the 1990-91 season in the first League game played at Walsall's brand new Bescot Stadium.

For Torquay, it was a dream start. They remained unbeaten for the first fourteen games of the season, topping the table, although Saunders picked up an injury in mid-September, forcing him to miss eight games.

His return coincided with United's first defeat, at Scarborough, and suddenly the confidence evaporated from the side. The situation was not helped by injuries to several key players. Smith brought in a number of other signings, but results were such that, by early April, United found themselves in the bottom half of the table. An increasingly fraught relationship with his chairman saw Smith surprisingly resign, with assistant John Impey taking over.

Saunders, captaining the side, was proving to be an influential figure. He knew just one way to play the game – with 100 per cent commitment, and expected nothing less from his team-mates. Inevitably, he upset a few people on the way. One well-publicised incident involved a dispute with veteran striker Tommy Tynan, who was player-coach at the time.

In a hotel, a few senior players were playing cards. Fuelled by alcohol, events took a turn for the worst. A fight broke out and Saunders ended up punching Tynan, giving him a black eye. Later, Tynan went to Saunders' room to 'discuss' the incident. A further brawl ensued, during which Tynan picked up a kettle and hit Saunders with it. An internal disciplinary hearing lay the blame squarely with Tynan, who never played for the club again, whilst Saunders was exonerated.

Under Impey, United's form returned and they scraped into the final play-off spot. A 2-1 aggregate win over Burnley clinched a Wembley place against Blackpool. After extra-time, the scores were tied at 2-2 and, with the penalty shoot-out standing at 4-4, Blackpool striker Dave Bamber shot wide to hand United their first promotion for nineteen years.

The excitement of the new season soon waned. United quickly slumped to the bottom of the table. By early October, Impey was sacked and Saunders given the role of caretaker manager. A change of leader failed to change fortunes. Wins were hard to come by and United were knocked out of the FA Cup by Farnborough.

Playing-wise, Saunders was sidelined by a knee injury anyway, and did not return until February, by which time Ivan Golac found himself in the hot seat. Saunders' failure to produce results had cost him the chance of landing the manager's job on a permanent basis. Saunders returned to playing, but his return failed to galvanise the side and an inevitable relegation followed.

Saunders started the first seven games of the new season, even scoring a hat-trick against Hereford in the Coca-Cola Cup, but the knee ligament damage was still troubling him. He made a brief return for one game in March, but the injury finally forced his retirement from the professional game.

He returned to the North East, playing for Spennymoor before managing a number of teams locally, as well as working in the family textile business.

Despite his relatively brief Torquay career, Saunders was highly regarded at the club and his leadership qualities had played a big part in the Wembley triumph. In 1997, he made a return to Plainmoor when the club staged a testimonial on his behalf. A Torquay XI took on a 'Premier XI' containing several of Saunders' former Newcastle team-mates, such as Paul Gascoigne, Peter Beardsley and Chris Waddle. A highly respectable crowd of 5,770 witnessed an entertaining if not ultra competitive game, which the Premier side won 8-6. Many thought it was the last they would see of Saunders at Plainmoor but, in the summer of 1998, chairman Bateson turned to him again when Kevin Hodges was given the opportunity to manage Plymouth.

United had made good progress under Hodges' stewardship, having again made the play-off finals at Wembley, where they were defeated by Colchester. Of course, the fans were optimistic that the club could continue to progress, but Saunders had inherited a weakened squad, most notably by the departure of Rodney Jack, but also by the loss of other solid performers such as defenders, Jon Gittens (to Exeter) and Paul Gibbs, who had followed Hodges to Plymouth.

After an encouraging two wins in the first three matches, form went out the window, with just one win in the next seventeen games. Keeper Matthew Gregg was sold to Crystal Palace for £400,000, and experienced central defender Alex Watson, who was also Saunders' assistant, was sidelined by injury.

In late September, Saunders pulled off something of a coup by persuading his good friend, England international Chris Waddle, to sign. The trusty left foot was still capable of displaying the occasional genius, but Waddle lasted just seven games before taking a coaching position with Sheffield Wednesday.

In December, another multi-capped international joined, in the considerable shape of goalkeeper Neville Southall. Agile and mobile he was not, but he still made the art of goalkeeping look ridiculously easy at times. His arrival sparked a mini revival, which eventually saw United pull clear of the relegation zone, but it was the not the sort of season anyone, particularly Saunders, was happy with. He knew that a poor start to the following campaign would see him on borrowed time.

Most of the expectations for the new season were firmly on the shoulders of striker Eifion Williams. The Welsh striker had been signed from Barry Town for a club record £70,000 towards the end of the previous season, and had scored a debut hat-trick. In tandem with Tony Bedeau, it was hoped that the duo would score enough goals to secure success. In fairness, they did manage 26 league goals between them, but a poor mid-season run of form cost United dearly and they managed a ninth-place finish, just three points shy of a play-off place.

Early optimism for the 2000-01 season quickly evaporated. One goal and one point from the first four games was not what the doctor had ordered. Worse was to follow, with a 2-6 defeat at Brighton. A run of six successive defeats saw United slump to the bottom and Saunders was a man under pressure. A misfiring forward line was not helping matters.

Results did not improve, despite efforts to strengthen the squad and the predictable tinkering of line ups and formations. By the end of February, chairman Bateson brought in Colin Lee as a consultant to help Saunders. From that moment the writing was on the wall and inevitably, within a couple of weeks, with United bottom of the Football League, Saunders was sacked.

United escaped demotion, thanks to the infamous last-day victory at Barnet.

In time, Saunders became a football agent, representing his good mate, Paul Gascoigne, among others. More recently he has identified and recommended several foreign players to clubs. Most notably, he unearthed Egyptian striker Amir Zaki, who was an instant hit at Premiership side Wigan.

Magic Moment: *Saunders scored Torquay's opening goal in their Wembley play-off triumph with a brave header that typified his fearless approach to the game.*

Worst Nightmare: *Playing for Newcastle in a North East derby with Sunderland on New Year's Day 1985, Saunders found himself on the receiving end of an horrendous 'tackle' by Gary Bennett. Saunders escaped serious injury but Bennett was sent off.*

TORQUAY RECORD	Appearances	Goals
League	64	7
FA Cup	1	0
League Cup	5	4

No 44. **JUSTIN FASHANU**

Debut: v Preston, 20 December 1991
Farewell: v Doncaster, 26 January 1993

The choice of Justinus Soni Fashanu as one of United's 50 greatest will no doubt prove to be a controversial one, but Fashanu himself courted controversy throughout his life, and of the hundreds of players to have pulled on a Torquay United shirt, few have possessed more talent than him. His ability, however, was overshadowed by a series of ultimately tragic events off the field.

Fashanu was born in Hackney, East London on 19 February 1961, the son of a Nigerian father – Patrick, and a Guyanese mother – Pearl. Sadly, when Justin was just four, his parents separated and he and his younger brother, John, were sent to a Barnardo's home in Barkingside, an institution designed to care for vulnerable children.

When he was six years old, Justin and John were fostered by Alf and Betty Jackson in the Norfolk village of Shropham near Attleborough. The brothers' introduction to life in 'middle England' was a far cry from their early years. Justin sang in the local church choir, but it was in sport where they both displayed their talents. Justin excelled in boxing, to the extent that he was tipped for a professional career in the ring. In March 1977, when he was sixteen, he lost the British Schoolboy Heavyweight final in Blackpool. The fact that he was fighting at this weight said a lot about the fine physique he possessed. At over six feet tall and with a highly toned body, he was a natural athlete. His prowess as a striker on the football field had been monitored by a number of clubs. He joined Norwich City at age fourteen, and in the end they lured him away from boxing and his first job as a steel erector to sign apprentice forms at Carrow Road in September 1977.

He progressed quickly, being selected for the England youth team and signing as a professional in December 1978, making his league debut seventeen days later. He quickly established himself in the side and began earning rave reviews and, subsequently, eleven England Under-21 caps. His powerful frame made him a difficult man to mark and he was capable of the unusual and unexpected. If there was a weakness in his game it was his occasional lack of discipline. Fashanu was dismissed in one match for allegedly kicking Aston Villa defender Allan Evans, which provoked crowd trouble, in which Villa keeper Jimmy Rimmer was hit by a coin, forcing both managers to appeal for calm before the game could continue.

Whilst at Norwich he also had loan spells with Australian club, Adelaide City.

Despite his occasional indiscretions, Fashanu was one of the bright young stars of English football and was linked with a number of 'big' clubs. Norwich's relegation at the end of the 1980-81 season made his departure inevitable, and it was Nottingham Forest manager Brian Clough who signed him for £1 million. It seemed Fashanu had the world at his feet, but the move to the City Ground saw the start of his downfall. A combination of factors saw his time at Forest turn into a nightmare. Fashanu was confident and brash. So was Clough. The exuberant manager might have accepted his new centre-forward's attitude, had he been doing what he was paid for – scoring goals. But Fashanu found it difficult to adapt to both his new team's style of play and Clough's lifestyle demands on him, and the goals dried up. Clough also learned of rumours that Fashanu was frequenting gay clubs and bars. Fashanu's apparent sexuality was the final straw. Clough barred him from training with the side, loaned him to Southampton, and finally sold him to local rivals Notts County for a knockdown £150,000.

Fashanu rediscovered his scoring touch, but on New Year's Eve 1983 suffered a serious knee injury. He recovered, but not fully. He was sold to Brighton in June 1985 for £115,000, somehow passing his medical, but the injury restricted him to just sixteen games. Realising he would never attain past glories, Fashanu announced his retirement.

He went to the USA for surgery, which was seemingly successful, prompting thoughts of a comeback. Thus began a merry-go-round of clubs. In the States he played for Los Angeles Heat before moving to Canada with Edmonton Brickmen and then Hamilton Steelers.

In October 1989, he returned to these shores, playing twice for Manchester City, then to West Ham, a trial with Ipswich, and also appearing for Leyton Orient, all within the space of five months. It didn't stop there. He joined non-league Southall as player-coach, returned to Canada with Toronto Blizzard, and signed semi-professional terms for Leatherhead.

It seemed no one really wanted to take a risk on Fashanu. He made one substitute appearance for Newcastle, but manager Ossie Ardiles refused to offer him a contract.

On 23 November 1991, Fashanu arrived at Plainmoor. It was perhaps a sign of the desperate times at Torquay that they were prepared to gamble on him. They looked cast-iron certs for relegation, had sacked manager John Impey in October after a dismal start and, a week before Fashanu's debut, popular defender John Uzzell had suffered a sickening head injury which would ultimately end his career and result in court action.

The transfer at least gave Torquay some publicity and Fashanu was certainly not publicity shy. He had already openly admitted his homosexuality and now embarked on a short-lived and unlikely relationship with Coronation Street actress Julie Goodyear, better known to the nation as the leopardskin-clad barmaid, Bet Lynch.

Back on the field, Fashanu seemed to settle at Torquay, compared to his previous nomadic existence, and at least found the net on a reasonably regular basis, a concept his team-mates had failed to grasp. In February 1992, Ivan Golac was appointed as the new manager and gave Fashanu the role of his assistant. Fash's ten goals in 21 appearances easily made him the club's top scorer, but relegation could not be avoided, costing Golac his job, although Fashanu retained his assistant's role to new boss Paul Compton. Fashanu still found himself in trouble though. Near the end of the season, he received a £265 fine and a 28-day driving ban for speeding and failing to produce his driving licence.

The new season saw Fashanu return, but Torquay's form didn't. Another relegation battle ensued, with Conference football looking a distinct possibility. There was also a dreadful 2-5 FA Cup defeat by non-league Yeovil.

The experienced Neil Warnock was brought in as a consultant to help Compton, who was ultimately dismissed. Fashanu applied for the managerial vacancy but it was no surprise that Warnock was given the job. Fashanu left the club to embark on another world tour, which took in clubs in Scotland (Airdrie and Hearts), Sweden, Australia, New Zealand and USA. His contract at Hearts was terminated following his false press allegations of 'encounters' with cabinet ministers.

Aged 37, Fashanu announced his retirement as a player. He went to Maryland, USA, claiming he was the coach of the local side, the Mania, although it subsequently emerged that he was only being considered for the position and no contracts had been signed. It was here that the final spiral in his life began. On 25 March 1998, he was accused of sexually assaulting a seventeen-year-old boy. He was questioned by police and within days had fled back to England.

On the morning of 3 May, he was found hanged in a deserted lock-up garage in Shoreditch, London. He had broken in, the last act of a tragic life. But the tragedy did not end there. In his suicide note he stated that 'I realised that I had already been presumed guilty'. But he had not. At a later inquest it was heard that the American police had dropped their investigation due to lack of evidence.

Magic Moment: *A spectacular turn and long-range volley against Liverpool earned Fashanu the BBC 'Goal of the Season' award in 1980.*

Worst Nightmare: *During his one Newcastle appearance, the dressing room was burgled with Fashanu losing money and jewellery.*

TORQUAY RECORD	Appearances	Goals
League	41	15
FA Cup	1	0
League Cup	3	2

No 45. **DARREN MOORE**

Debut: v Birmingham, 24 March 1992
Farewell: v Gillingham, 6 May 1995

Appearances can be deceptive. Darren Mark Moore is living proof of that old adage. At 6ft 3ins and over 15st, his muscular frame cuts an intimidating figure. Yet, off the field, Moore is one of the nicest people in football and one who, as we shall see, gives a lot of his time and effort to worthy causes.

There are, I suspect, a number of centre-forwards who may not necessarily agree with my perceptions. Once he crosses the touchline, Moore transforms into a no-nonsense, physical defender who has regularly incurred the wrath of various officials over the years. Much of this can be put down to his understandable lack of mobility and speed, rather than any premeditated nastiness. He can also play a bit, as his lengthy and successful career suggests.

Moore was born of Jamaican parentage in Birmingham on 22 April 1974. He attended James Watt school in Handsworth and was an avid Aston Villa fan, idolising Paul McGrath, who knew a thing or two about defending himself.

Moore attributes his start in football to Jean Bell, a school caretaker, who also ran a football team. She recommended him to Normanhurst Villa, and Moore continued to climb the football ladder from there. Typically, he has not forgotten his roots, staying in touch with her and revisiting his old school.

He joined Holly Lane Colts and went to Walsall as a schoolboy but that didn't work out. He was also a promising all-rounder at cricket.

The Holly Lane goalkeeper had a trial at Torquay and Moore followed, confessing that, at first, he did not even know where Torquay was, but he impressed sufficiently to be taken on as a trainee.

His early experiences were not happy. He was homesick and was subjected to racial abuse from some senior trainees but, showing a resolve that has served him well, Moore knuckled down.

The 1991-92 season saw Torquay embroiled in a Division Three relegation battle. New manager Ivan Golac had failed to halt the slide and had lost centre-half Matt Elliott to Scunthorpe on loan. With another central defender, Chris Curran, injured, Moore – still a trainee – was thrown into the lions' den for a challenging debut against second-placed Birmingham. City won 2-1 but Moore was given another chance when he was recalled for the final four games of the season, scoring against Bolton, but by this stage relegation was inevitable.

In November 1992 'Bruno', as he was nicknamed, due to his likeness to the boxer of the same name, was given a professional contract, having already established himself as United's first-choice centre-half, his height and power well suited to the unsophisticated, direct style of the newly named Division Three (still the fourth tier of English football). He made such an impact that he was voted United's 'Player of the Year' at the end of the 1992-93 season.

Moore's physical presence was also a factor at set-pieces and perhaps he should have scored more often than he did. One of his most memorable goals, however, was not a header, but a stunning volley in the first leg of the 1994 play-off semi-final at home to Preston.

Moore was gaining a burgeoning reputation, with several bigger clubs showing an interest in him, but Torquay slapped a huge fee in front of any potential suitors. Moore, however, had ambitions to further his career, so a move to Third Division rivals Doncaster in July 1995 seemed a strange one. Neither club could agree a transfer fee, and so an independent tribunal set it at £62,500, a record for Rovers.

It was not that Moore was unhappy at Plainmoor, but he felt that a move to Yorkshire would put him in a more visible shop window. He was right. After two seasons at Rovers, he clinched a £310,000 transfer to Bradford City.

His first season was blighted by injury, but the year after, he missed just two games as the Bantams clinched promotion to the Premiership under Paul Jewell. Moore seemed to be on the cusp of achieving his ambition of playing top-flight football, but things turned sour when the club insisted that every player either signed a new contract or did not play. Moore was not happy with the terms, or the way it was handled, and found himself frozen out. He was transfer-listed without being told, and could not even get a game in the reserves.

Eventually, Portsmouth manager Alan Ball offered him an escape route for a fee of £500,000. They were difficult times at Fratton Park but, as ever, Moore concentrated on his football, winning his three Jamaican caps whilst there, although he is convinced he has played in several more friendlies for the 'Reggae Boyz'.

In September 2001 he returned to the Midlands to sign for West Brom in a £750,000 deal. He was a rock at the heart of their defence, helping them win promotion to the Premiership and named in the PFA divisional team of the year.

The Baggies' first game in the Premiership was at Old Trafford. Moore had finally realised his dream. Sadly, Albion dropped straight back down but instantly gained promotion again.

Moore was far from being a regular in that 2005-06 season, and in the January was sent off in a game against Wigan. It was to be his last game for Albion. A few weeks later, he signed for Derby.

Moore's promotion magic worked again when Derby clinched a Premiership spot after a bitter-sweet victory over West Brom in the play-off final the following season. He was again named in the PFA divisional side.

Derby's foray into the Premiership was a disaster from the off, and they finished well adrift at the bottom. Despite this, Moore's efforts were appreciated by his colleagues who voted him their 'Player's Player of the Year'.

Following relegation, it looked likely that Moore would return to Bradford, but he eventually signed for Barnsley and remains a regular in the heart of their defence.

Despite his football commitments, Moore manages to find time to devote to various causes. He is a devout Christian and involved in the 'Faith and Football' movement, along with other pros such as Lua Lua, Linvoy Primus, and Rory Fallon. In 2005 he and Primus walked the Great Wall of China to raise money for charity, and he is a great supporter of Christian Aid and Oxfam. He is a prime mover in the 'Let's Kick Racism Out of Football' campaign and currently serves on the PFA management committee. He is also a qualified coach to boot, and will surely put his experience to good use in the game for many years to come.

Magic Moment: *In November 2004, Moore was 'shocked and surprised' to receive an award for his 'outstanding contribution to Grass Roots and Community Football Projects'.*

Worst Nightmare: *In the second leg of the 1994 play-off semi-final at Deepdale, Moore was sent off in the 36th minute for allegedly striking Preston forward Paul Raynor. It was the turning point of the game, with North End narrowly going through to Wembley on aggregate, thanks to a winner from Raynor, who was later disciplined for 'play acting'.*

TORQUAY RECORD	Appearances	Goals
League	105	9
FA Cup	7	1
League Cup	6	0

No 46. **DON O'RIORDAN**

Debut: v Cardiff, 13 February 1993
Farewell: v Scunthorpe, 28 October 1995

Donald Joseph O'Riordan was one of the most skilful players on Torquay's books in recent times. He had a successful career in the lower leagues and, although he was at the veteran stage when he was a Gull, the United fans still saw his talent.

O'Riordan was born in Ballyfermot, Dublin, on 14 May 1957. The curly haired, fresh-faced youngster was brought to Derby as an apprentice, turning professional in July 1975.

He showed considerable promise at the Baseball Ground and was equally comfortable as a midfield player or central defender, making his first-team debut in March 1977 as an early substitute for the injured Charlie George in a 0-0 draw at Spurs. He won Irish Youth international honours to add to his Irish Schoolboy caps. He would eventually also play once for the Irish Under-21 side.

O'Riordan found it tough to break into the Derby starting eleven. He made a total of just seven appearances (five as substitute), scoring once. In January 1978 he spent a brief period on loan at Doncaster, playing twice, but a month later was given a free transfer by Derby boss, Tommy Docherty, and joined Tulsa Roughnecks in the USA.

O'Riordan's transfer was one of a number to American clubs in that period, and was the subject of an overall police investigation into the financial affairs of the club at that time.

Although the US soccer scene was taking off in the late 1970s, it was usually a graveyard for players trying to eke out a couple more years of their career. For O'Riordan it was the opportunity to gain valuable experience and, although he was one of the youngest Roughnecks, he was the only one to play in every game of the NASL season.

With the American season at an end, O'Riordan was transferred to Preston for a fee of £30,000. He spent a second season at Tulsa, but it was at Deepdale where he really found his feet, playing over 150 games and being voted the Player of the Year in 1981-82.

In August 1983 he moved to Carlisle, again for a fee of £30,000 and spent two years before he was on the move again, this time to Middlesbrough, who paid £55,000 for him. Again he featured regularly, but with dire financial problems at Ayresome Park, O'Riordan was one of a number of players released.

He was courted by a number of clubs but joined Grimsby, tempted by the added sweetener of a player-assistant manager role. It was a turbulent time at Grimsby. Relegation cost manager Mike Lyons his job. O'Riordan remained as assistant to new boss Bobby Roberts, but he too was dismissed following a second successive relegation. O'Riordan was offered the role of player-manager but declined, instead opting for a transfer to Notts County.

The transfer fee of £16,000 was eventually set by a tribunal. O'Riordan went to Meadow Lane, expecting to manage the reserves. He was now in his 30s but enjoyed a second wind. The 1990-91 season was a particularly memorable one. He scored with a stunning 25-yard strike in an FA Cup quarter-final at Tottenham, and at the end of the season he found himself on a winning side at Wembley, when County defeated Brighton to seal promotion the First Division under the guidance of manager Neil Warnock.

To play top-flight football at such a late stage was something of a fairy tale, especially when County's opening fixture took them to Old Trafford. But there the fairy tale ended. O'Riordan suffered an Achilles injury in that game which ended his season, with surgery eventually required.

To no one's surprise, County were immediately relegated, albeit having gathered a respectable 40 points. Warnock was sacked halfway into the following season, when County had managed just four wins.

Torquay chairman Mike Bateson moved quickly, inviting Warnock to come to Plainmoor as a management consultant to aid rookie boss Paul Compton, who had seen his side slump to the bottom of the division and suffer heavy losses in both cup competitions. Warnock wasted no time in bringing four Notts County players to Plainmoor, including O'Riordan. Within two months, Compton returned to his previous youth development role, leaving Warnock in sole charge.

The new faces certainly helped bring some improvement to results. O'Riordan, in particular, was a major influence on the side. His experience and competitive edge proved invaluable. He was a lovely passer of the ball and read the game well. There were the occasional flashes of Irish temper, but he was quickly forgiven by the United faithful. In the end, United lost just two of their final nine games to avoid relegation to non-league football.

In the summer, Warnock departed, tempted by the offer of the manager's job at Huddersfield. Despite the plethora of applications that any vacancy brings, the board offered the job to O'Riordan which he accepted gratefully.

He must have thought the management lark was easy when he went undefeated in his first eight games in charge. O'Riordan continued to play as well, either in midfield or as a sweeper. United's form ebbed and flowed during the season, but they managed to finish in a play-off position before losing in controversial circumstances to Preston.

After a mid-table finish in 1994-95, O'Riordan's side started the following campaign poorly. He had been handicapped by the loss of some of his better players. Darren Moore, Paul Trollope and Gregory Goodridge had all been sold for decent money, but had not been adequately replaced. On the back of this, crowds had slumped to the 2,000-mark and O'Riordan was a man under increasing pressure.

That pressure became unbearable when, after conceding four against both Barnet and Plymouth in successive games, United lost 1-8 at home to Scunthorpe, a record defeat for the club. At the final whistle, the home fans, those that were left anyway, demonstrated against, well, pretty much everything. O'Riordan's dismissal was inevitable and, sure enough, it was confirmed a few hours later.

It was a sad end to his Torquay career. The manner and scale of the defeat overshadowed his overall contribution to the cause and, sadly, his name will always be associated with that defeat.

O'Riordan went to Scarborough but played just once to bring the curtain down on his English League career. He also played for Gloucester City and Dorchester before eventually returning to Ireland in the summer of 1997 to manage and, occasionally play for, Galway United. In May 2001 he was sacked, the victim of a cost-cutting exercise. Two months later, he was appointed manager of Sligo Rovers.

When Warnock was manager of Sheffield United, O'Riordan was reacquainted with his former boss. He was asked to join the club's youth set up, and in recent times has been working in China where he has helped to establish a youth academy for the Blades.

Magic Moment: *In 1988, O'Riordan, then a Grimsby player, was voted the 'Third Division Defender of the Year' by the Sunday People newspaper.*

Worst Nightmare: *Although not a prolific scorer, by any means, O'Riordan scored twice past future England keeper Nigel Martyn for Grimsby against Bristol Rovers, but was denied a memorable hat-trick when he hit the post.*

TORQUAY RECORD	Appearances	Goals
League	79	3
FA Cup	5	0
League Cup	3	0

No 47. **TONY BEDEAU**

Debut: v Cardiff, 8 September 1995
Farewell: v Crawley (Conference), 26 April 2008

It is difficult to believe that Anthony Charles Osmond Bedeau is only just into his 30s. That is not being unkind; it is just that he seems to have been a Torquay player for many years.

Bedeau was handed his United debut by manager Don O'Riordan at the age of just sixteen, when he was still a first year YTS player. It was a particularly productive year for the youth players, as fellow trainees Matthew Gregg, Wayne Thomas and Garry Monk also made their first-team bows during that season.

Bedeau was born in Hammersmith, London, on 24 March 1979. He attended Chiswick School and played for the school, borough, and county teams. Having reached this level, he naturally came to the attention of a number of professional clubs and opted to join Arsenal. He then moved to Chelsea where he played at Under-14 level.

Having been discarded by the Blues, Bedeau came to Torquay for trials. He has to thank Kevin Hodges, then youth-team coach, for his opportunity. Hodges was impressed by the young striker, particularly his blistering pace, and recommended him to O'Riordan.

O'Riordan departed not long after Bedeau's debut, although he was given another two substitute outings by new boss Eddie May before making his full debut in the penultimate game of the season against Cambridge. Torquay were already doomed to finish bottom, and were saved from relegation only by the inadequacies of Stevenage's stadium.

The dire form of that season saw May leave and Hodges given the opportunity to take charge of the first team. With Rodney Jack and mid-season signing, Andy McFarlane being the first-choice forward line, Bedeau again found his opportunities restricted, but he made eight appearances and scored his first goal in the last game of the season against Doncaster.

With an impressive two-year apprenticeship at an end, Bedeau was taken on as a professional, and the 1997-98 season saw him regularly involved with the first-team squad, albeit largely as a substitute. He featured in 41 games, including coming on as a replacement for the veteran Steve McCall in the Wembley play-off defeat to Colchester.

Bedeau soon became a permanent fixture in the Gulls' line up, and his lively, strong play and pace soon made him a favourite with the crowd. He also began to find the net on a regular basis, and in the 1999-2000 season finished as the club's top scorer with seventeen goals.

His impressive performances soon captured the attention of other sides. On the recommendation of Chris Waddle, he spent a week training with Sheffield Wednesday, who were impressed sufficiently to offer Torquay £50,000. Torquay were not so impressed, and turned the offer down.

The 2000-01 season was particularly eventful. Bedeau missed the early games through injury but scored three times in his first two games back. He was also gaining a reputation as United's danger-man, and accordingly received some rough treatment from opponents. Bedeau himself was in regular trouble with the officials, notching up five yellow cards in his first eight games and eleven in total during the season. This was not deterring other sides from trying to prise him away from Plainmoor. He spent a week on trial at Sunderland, and no sooner had he returned to Devon than United received an offer of £200,000 from Oxford, then a First Division side. Two months later an unlikely bid of £150,000 came from Rochdale. Bedeau travelled to Spotland for discussions but decided that a move north was not for him.

The speculation and uncertainty seemed to unsettle him. He scored just four more times that season, although he was used more in a wide role as the season went on.

Roy McFarland's tenure as Torquay manager coincided with one of Bedeau's unhappiest spells at Plainmoor. He found himself in and out of the side and, in January 2002, joined Barnsley on loan, making three substitute appearances for the Oakwell side.

Bedeau returned to Plainmoor and quickly regained his place in the side. He describes his proudest moment as being part of the Torquay squad that was promoted in 2003-04, and his worst as the following season when United were immediately relegated again.

The latter days of Bedeau's United career were spent playing in a variety of positions, including full-back and midfield. Yet that relegation season cried out for the Bedeau of old, when goals were at a premium.

The 2005-06 season saw him finish as top scorer again, with eleven goals, but at the end of that campaign he joined Walsall on a free transfer. Bedeau believed he needed a fresh challenge after so long at one club, but the move to the relatively plush surroundings of the Bescot Stadium did not work out as he had hoped. He struggled to find a team place and, in February 2007, had another three-game loan spell, this time at Bury.

At the end of that season he was transfer-listed and made a nostalgic return to Plainmoor on a twelve-month contract. He played 24 games in that season, which was interspersed with a nine-game loan at Weymouth, but at the end of the season finally ended his long association with Torquay when he was released.

He briefly played for Kingstonian during the following season, but now has returned permanently to London and admits that his football days are now behind him.

Magic Moment: *At the age of just 26, Bedeau had racked up ten years' service at Torquay and was awarded a testimonial. Local rivals Plymouth Argyle provided the pre-season opposition in July 2005.*

Worst Nightmare: *In November 2001 Bedeau and fellow striker David Graham were transfer-listed by Roy McFarland for 'general lack of effort and passion'.*

TORQUAY RECORD	Appearances	Goals
League	330	58
FA Cup	20	3
League Cup	9	3

No 48. **RODNEY JACK**

Debut: v Preston, 14 October 1995
Farewell: v Colchester (play-off final), 22 May 1998

There have been few more exciting sights for a Torquay fan in modern times than to watch the fleet-footed Rodney Jack in full flow. He will be remembered with great affection for many years.

Jack – middle name 'Alphonso' – was born in Kingstown on the Caribbean island of St Vincent on 28 September 1972. By the time he had reached his teenage years, Jack, with his natural speed and athleticism, was showing a talent for football on this cricket-mad island.

He eventually signed for Lambada FC, which was owned and managed by Kevin Millard, an exiled Gulls fan who had been a previous coach of Barbados. Millard had already been responsible for sending Gregory Goodridge, another fondly remembered, exciting player to Plainmoor, where his talents resulted in a £100,000 move to QPR.

In August 1995, Millard brought his Lambada side to England, in a move partly designed to showcase his best talent. The tour involved a friendly at Plainmoor. On a balmy August day, Jack immediately caught the eye. He was short and frail-looking, but blisteringly quick. The Torquay defenders had no answer to his pace. It was not just the sparse crowd who were impressed. Afraid that his ability would be spotted elsewhere, chairman Mike Bateson immediately started the process to make him a Torquay player.

With work permits and other associated red tape to cut through, Jack eventually signed on the dotted line on 10 October. By this stage, Jack must have been wondering if he had made the right decision. That balmy August day had been replaced by the onset of a British winter. What was more, United were propping up the whole of the Football League, having won just two of their first eleven league games and suffered a 3-9 aggregate League Cup defeat to Norwich.

Within four days of signing, Jack was handed his debut. He was already the 22nd player-manager Don O'Riordan had used in an effort to find a winning formula.

Jack's debut ended in a 0-4 home defeat by Preston. This was followed by a 3-4 loss at Plymouth and a horrendous 1-8 thrashing at home by the might of Scunthorpe, with Andy McFarlane, later to be a Gull, scoring four. This was the final straw for many supporters, who demonstrated after the game, prompting Bateson to sack O'Riordan before the day was out.

Mick Buxton was given temporary charge, and actually led United to a victory in the FA Cup at Leyton Orient, but it was Eddie May who was given the role permanently.

The form under May improved little. It would be late January before a league win came along, again against Orient, but one win and just six goals in the final twenty games condemned the side to inevitable relegation. Jack was one of the few players to show any sort of form during this dismal period, although inevitably he took time to settle into the English style of play and way of life.

Of course, history shows that United were saved from relegation to the Conference by a technicality when their replacements, Stevenage, were deemed to have a stadium not up to Football League requirements. An appeal against the decision also failed, and United were handed a reprieve.

Inevitably, May was soon gone, to be replaced by Kevin Hodges, Plymouth's record appearance holder, who had been seeing out his playing days at Plainmoor. He enlisted the help of his former team-mates, Steve McCall and Garry Nelson, who at least brought experience and guile to the club. Despite their advancing years, both could still play a bit as well.

Fortunes improved little on the pitch, however. The management team faced financial restraints, disciplinary problems, and lack of general resources, to name but a few challenges, all of which were beautifully described in Nelson's subsequent book *Left Foot In The Grave*. Jack was one of the few successes of the campaign, finishing as top scorer and scaring Third Division defenders to death with his direct style. His stock was rising, other clubs were taking note, and it seemed only a matter of time before a move elsewhere would beckon. In October 1996, Jack spent a week training with Newcastle, but the proposed move to the North East fell through.

There was also the novelty of seeing a Torquay player regularly disappearing for international duty. Jack won fifteen caps for St Vincent whilst a Gull, a club record, and won 45 caps in total.

Despite the struggles, Hodges remained in charge and recruited several new players. The combination clicked and the transformation was remarkable. United were suddenly promotion contenders. Jack was, by now, a marked man, but few defenders got the better of him. A masterstroke was the arrival of striker Jason Roberts, on loan from Wolves, in December 1997. He and Jack formed an instant understanding and United set a new club record of eight successive wins which lifted them to second. Roberts' loan spell ended, he returned to Wolves, and then was loaned out again, this time to Bristol City. His departure from Torquay seemed to knock the stuffing out of the side and there was a sudden loss of form, which culminated in automatic promotion being missed but the lottery of a play-off place secured.

United's play-off opponents were Scarborough, who had run out 4-1 victors in a league encounter in January, but Hodges' charges were now made of sterner stuff, and Jack in particular was on fire for both legs, scoring three times in a 7-2 aggregate victory to seal a Wembley appearance against Colchester.

The U's were a doughty side and included Paul Buckle, a future United player and manager. There was heartache for Torquay as Colchester scored the only goal through a controversial penalty.

Jack's Wembley appearance was his final bow in a Torquay shirt. It was a surprise that he had not been tempted elsewhere already, but no one had predicted that his destination would be Crewe. Although a First Division side, they were hardly considered as big spenders, preferring to nurture their own talent, but shelled out £650,000 to secure Jack's services, easily a record fee for both clubs.

Jack soon thrilled the Gresty Road faithful, scoring some stunning long-range goals, with one particular spectacular solo effort against Cheltenham remaining long in the memory. After Crewe were relegated, he played a major role in securing an instant return to Division One when his sixteen goals helped the Alex to a runners-up spot behind Wigan in 2002-03.

Jack then rejected a new two-year contract and joined Rushden & Diamonds, but relegation and financial problems hit the Nene Park club. Manager Brian Talbot left for Oldham and Jack soon followed him. By this time, however, injuries and in particular a persistent hamstring problem, were taking their toll. He was released by Oldham and spent a brief spell in Ireland with Waterford.

In the summer of 2006, Jack received a hero's welcome when he rejoined Crewe, but he was not the same player and, after one season, was not offered a new contract. He joined non-league Southport and most recently has remained in the North West to play for Nantwich.

Magic Moment: *Jack played for Lambada in the* CONCACAF *Champions League final in front of 77,000 fans at Miami's Orange Bowl. His side lost 0-1 to Mexican champions, Necaxa.*

Worst Nightmare: *Jack scored after nineteen minutes in the Wembley play-off final against Colchester, only to have the effort ruled out for offside.*

TORQUAY RECORD	Appearances	Goals
League	90	27
FA Cup	6	0
League Cup	6	1

No 49. **KEVIN HILL**

Debut: v Macclesfield, 9 August 1997
Farewell: v Ebbsfleet, 10 May 2008

For managers, team-mates and supporters, Kevin Hill was the ideal player. Managers loved him, as he could run all day, score goals, create goals, tackle, take set-pieces, had great heading ability, and was a left-sided player. Team-mates loved him as he would work hard for the team and rarely waste a pass. Supporters loved him because of all of these, but they also realised his passion for the game and for the fact that Hill also appreciated the fans and always had time for them.

'Hilly's' work ethic stems from the fact that he was grateful for the chance to play League football. He earned his opportunity the hard way. It was not the standard route for him. He was stacking shelves in a supermarket and playing local football when he was given his chance.

Born on 6 March 1976 and brought up in Budleigh Salterton, Hill was football mad as a youngster. His father was a good local player and admits to the fact that although Kevin was born on a Saturday morning he still managed to play that afternoon.

Kevin played his senior football initially at nearby Exmouth Town. It was during a Western League match against Torrington that their manager, the former Plymouth player and manager John Hore, spotted him and eventually persuaded the eighteen-year-old to join him at Torrington. Hore liked what he saw and promised Hill that he if he worked hard he would try to fix him up with a League club.

After two seasons at Torrington, when he scored 35 goals as a wing-back, Hore kept to his word and arranged a trial at Sunderland, where Hore's good friend Bobby Saxton was involved on the coaching side. Sunderland were impressed, but it was decided that Hill would be better off at a local club, and Hore informed Gulls manager Kevin Hodges of Hill's potential.

Hodges admits that he watched Hill three times and was in two minds whether to sign him. Fortunately for Torquay, he did in the summer of

1997. It was hardly a signing to get the fans in a lather. Many players had come from local football, played the odd game here and there, but drifted back from whence they came. But Hill impressed pre-season and was included as a substitute for the opening game of the season, coming on for the final twelve minutes for his debut.

The rest, as they say, is history. For the next ten years Hill never played fewer than 40 games a season. Those statistics bear testimony not only to his consistency in a period when the football club saw high and lows, but also to his levels of fitness. Hill would run all day. As a child he was hyper active and that has seemingly never left him. A favourite crowd chant would be: 'He's here, he's there, he's every ******* where, Kevin Hill, Kevin Hill.' Yes, he had his fair share of injuries, but they had to be serious to keep him out of the team.

He would also chip in with his fair share of goals, many with his head. For someone who measured under 6ft, he posed a huge aerial threat. He would leap like a salmon with seemingly spring-heeled boots.

His popularity with the supporters was not just borne from his performances on the field. Unlike the majority of present-day players who give the crowd a quick wave, have a shower and jump in the car, Hill was always willing to mingle with the fans, before and after a game. He was usually last off the pitch at the final whistle, making sure he acknowledged each section of United supporters.

Of all his notable performances, one incident remains in the memory. At an inhospitable, windswept Plainmoor on New Year's Day 2005, United entertained bottom of the table Stockport. County's keeper, Neil Cutler, gathered the ball and, as his defenders and, so he thought, the Torquay forwards dispersed, he rolled the ball on to the ground to effect his clearance. What he did not realise was that Hill was lurking furtively behind him. As soon as the ball was released, Hill nipped around the keeper, had time for a quick change of direction, and rolled the ball into an unguarded net.

During his United career, Hill played in a variety of positions. The majority were as a left-sided midfield player, but he also appeared at full-back, central defence, central midfield, and as a striker, where he had an impressive strike rate. With his all-action, battling style and eager tackling, there were a fair share of yellow cards but never a red.

In July 2007, Hill's long service was rightly rewarded with a testimonial against Plymouth Argyle.

With Hill rarely out of the side, he was beginning to threaten Dennis Lewis's long-standing club appearance record. But, in what turned out to be Hill's final season, he found himself more and more on the sidelines and the games began to run out. He equalled Lewis's record when he appeared in the second leg of the Conference play-off semi-finals at Plainmoor against local rivals Exeter. He scored United's only goal in a devastating 1-4 defeat that denied the Gulls a play-off final spot, after having won the first leg 2-1 at Exeter. Fortunately for him, United made it through to the FA Trophy final at Wembley, against Ebbsfleet. Hill was named on the bench, but with Ebbsfleet one up and the clock ticking away, Hill was sent on to break the record, taking into account all United first-team matches. Sadly for him, the score remained the same and it was a heartbreaking way to end his United career.

Hill had not started with United until the age of 21. One wonders how many appearances he would have clocked up had he broken into the side three or four years earlier. What is for sure is that there have been few more popular players to pull on a United shirt. If football had more players with the attitude of Kevin Hill, the game would be in a far better state.

Following his release by United, Hill signed for Dorchester Town on a two-year contract in June 2008.

Magic Moment: *Prior to his testimonial match, Hill's loyal service was acknowledged in a congratulatory letter from FIFA President Sepp Blatter.*

Worst Nightmare: *Despite having played in the majority of games during the season, Hill was left on the bench for United's 1998 play-off final against Colchester at Wembley. Manager Kevin Hodges opted to play more experienced players. Hill did not get on.*

TORQUAY RECORD	Appearances	Goals
League	418	52
FA Cup	26	2
League Cup	14	1

No 50. **CHRIS HARGREAVES**

Debut: v Grays, 12 August 2007
Farewell: n/a – still at club

'There's only one Chris Hargreaves.' That may well be the case, but watch any Torquay match and you would be forgiven for thinking a twin brother was also playing. Wherever the action is, the long-haired, muscular frame of the current Torquay captain seems to be in the thick of it.

A study of Hargreaves' career statistics would probably put him firmly in the 'journeyman' category. After all, he has spent the bulk of his twenty-year career in the lower divisions, although his ability was surely worthy of a higher stage. But the journeyman label is not one that he likes, and rightly so. There is far more to Christian Hargreaves than just a run-of-the-mill lower league player who covers every blade of grass.

'Greavesie' or 'Tarzan', as he is known in the dressing room, in deference to his long hair and highly toned physique, was born in Cleethorpes on 12 May 1972. He attended Lindsey School but it was at Everton where he first sniffed the possibility of becoming a pro when he joined the Goodison Park side as a schoolboy.

Aged fourteen, Hargeaves left Merseyside to return 'home' to join local side Grimsby as a trainee in June 1988. He signed a professional contract in December 1989 and soon made his mark when he came off the bench for his debut to score in a 2-0 home win over Gillingham.

In his early days, Hargreaves was actually a forward. His relationship with Grimsby manager Alan Buckley could be described as fractious at times. Hargreaves was on the end of many a verbal blast from the boss, but Buckley also had some regard for Hargreaves' natural ability, once telling him that he could be Grimsby's first £1 million player. Nevertheless, the majority of Hargreaves' 64 appearances for the Mariners came as a substitute.

After a brief loan spell at Scarborough, Hargreaves moved to Hull for £50,000 in July 1993. He spent two years there before moving again, this time to West Brom on a free transfer, where the manager was none other than Alan Buckley!

The spell at the Hawthorns was not particularly memorable, with just two first-team appearances (against Sunderland as a substitute in the league and Brescia in the Anglo-Italian Cup), and within six months another free transfer took him to Hereford.

In July 1998, he was on the move again, this time to newly relegated Plymouth. It was here that Hargreaves began to show his true ability, with some impressive displays from midfield, which had now become his established position. The crowd warmed to his energetic, forceful play and strong running. During his spell as a Pilgrim, Newcastle expressed an interest in signing him, but the club refused. 'It was not as if I needed the money,' says Hargreaves with typical humour. Another move to Reading also fell through after a dispute over the agent's fee.

After a two-year spell at Home Park, it was off to Northampton, where he enjoyed the luxury of a four-year stay, winning the club's Player of the Year award in 2001-02. It was then on to Brentford for a year, where he still managed to play 35 games, despite having a hernia operation, and notched up ten 'man of the match' awards. A five-hour daily commute understandably took its toll.

Next stop, Oxford, where he suffered the heartbreak of relegation to the Conference (sent down after defeat by promoted Leyton Orient, whom he nearly joined) and then defeat in the following season in the play-offs (on penalties).

And so, Hargreaves finally ended up at Plainmoor, signed by Paul Buckle in a new-look squad after the Gulls had suffered the ignominy of relegation to the Conference.

By this time, Hargreaves was 35. Many thought he would be a bit-part player. Nothing could be further from the truth. Possessing fitness levels that would put many a butcher's dog to shame, Hargreaves has proved indispensable in the heart of the United midfield. Never one to shirk a challenge, he is not the type to spray 60-yard passes around the pitch. Instead, he gets a foot in, breaks up the play, and dispenses a short pass to a team-mate. He is also strong in the air and possesses a powerful shot with that trusty left foot. After twenty years, he still admits that a defeat hits him hard, a testimony at least to his ongoing passion for the game and will to win.

He also seems to have found the answer to eternal youth. His dedication to training and maintaining a lifestyle that keeps him at the peak of physical fitness puts many younger players to shame. He retains the shoulder-length hair which has caused many an opposition fan to enquire of the whereabouts of his caravan.

It was fitting that it was Hargreaves who led his team-mates up the Wembley steps to collect the trophy after defeating Cambridge United in the Conference play-off final in May 2009. He had given a typical all-action display and scored a memorable goal to seal an unlikely return to League football at the age of 37.

Off the field, Hargreaves is an instantly likeable and personable figure. He possesses a great sense of humour and is also a dedicated family man with three children, having met his wife Fiona when he was a young Grimsby Town hopeful.

In recent times he has written a daily 'blog' on the local *Herald Express* newspaper website. The material has been put into book form – *Captain's Blog – Football, Fatherhood and the Fight for Promotion*, resulting in a highly entertaining and amusing insight into the daily life and (occasionally obscure) thoughts of a lower league footballer.

What of the future for Chris Hargreaves? He will probably carry on playing and playing, but he has taken his coaching badges and has helped out in a coaching capacity at Torquay. He has done some media work and his book has also unearthed another of his talents. Whatever he chooses, he will undoubtedly put his heart and soul into it.

It is perhaps fitting that Chris Hargreaves' profile concludes this tome. He epitomises what Torquay United is all about. Both he and United have spent their time in the lower leagues. They have both suffered low points, interspersed by a few highs, yet they remain friendly and upbeat. They possess never-say-die spirits that have seen them through adversity, and both will still hopefully be around for many years to come, to provide pleasure to the loyal fans that have followed them through thick and thin.

Magic Moment: *Hargreaves scored Torquay's opening goal in the 2009 play-off final victory at Wembley against Cambridge with a twenty-yard rising shot with his underused right foot.*

Worst Nightmare: *Hargreaves has scored just one own-goal in his career, but that was playing for Northampton against Manchester United in an FA Cup-tie. He sliced the ball past his own keeper in front of 10,000 watching supporters and a worldwide TV audience of approximately 60 million.*

TORQUAY RECORD (to 31/5/09)	Appearances	Goals
League (Conference)	87	9
FA Cup	6	0
FA Trophy	4	3

TORQUAY UNITED: 50 GOLDEN GREATS

160

LIST OF SUBSCRIBERS

Subscriber	*Favourite Player*
Steve Badcott	Jim McNichol
Paul Bastard	Robin Stubbs
BiXiE	
Rob Chidgey	Rodney Jack
Alan Childs	Robin Stubbs
Les Davies	Robin Stubbs
Robin Dredge (Geddington Gull)	Alan Smith
Terry George	Robin Stubbs
Simon 'Gillygull' Gillett	Alex Russell
Colin James Hall	Sammy Collins
Stan Henderson	Mark Loram
Gary Lane	Willie Brown
Stuart Latham	Garry Nelson
Jon Luxton	Dave Caldwell
Terry McElheron	Robin Stubbs
Luke Moss	Chris Hargreaves
Steve Mumford	Lee Sharpe
Graham Osborn	Dave Caldwell
Cliff Phillips	Don Mills
Darren Phillips	Rodney Jack
Andy Rennie	Alex Russell
Malcolm Rennie	Kevin Hill
Sam Robinson	David Graham
Steve Saunders	Steve Cooper
The Stoneman Family	Kevin Hill
J G Yeo	Robin Stubbs
www.1000flags.co.uk	Rodney Jack